Let It All Hang Out

Lettin

It

All

Hang

Out

RuPaul

An Autobiography

A *Warner* Book

First published in the United States of America by Hyperion 1995
First published in Great Britain by Warner Books 1995

Copyright © RuPaul 1995
A World of Wonder Book
Published by arrangement with Hyperion

The moral right of the author has been asserted.

Lyrics from "Carry On" by Martha Wash © 1992 Irving Music
Inc. & Eric Beall Music (BMI). All rights reserved.
International copyright secured. Used by permission.

Photo credits: Albert Sanchez (pp. ii. 1, 2, 4, 5, 6, 9, 10, 11, 13);
Margaret Parker (p. 60 [top]); Lahoma Van Zandt (pp. 62, 78);
Fabulous Rosser (p. 70); Exum (p. 77); Christopher Hedgepath
(p. 80); John Eder (pp. 84-85); Cherry Snow (pp. 87, 90); Paula
Gately Tillman (pp. 91, 98, 146); Alexis Di Biasio (pp. 99, 101,
123); Sindee (pp. 108, 109, 111, 125, 128, 129, 139, 140, 141,
142, 148, 150); Lizzerd Souffle Chalmers (p. 124); Jamie
McEwen (p. 130); Alison Pollet (p. 134); Joelle Pezely (p. 158);
Firooz Zahedi (p. 169); Jeff Kravitz (p. 187); Philip
Ollerenshaw (pp. 193, 195-198); Greg Gorman (p. 220); Gianni
Versace (p. 224). All others: The RuPaul Collection.

A CIP catalogue record for this book
is available from the British Library.

ISBN 0 7515 1587 6

Printed and bound in Great Britain by
BPC Consumer Books Ltd
A member of
The British Printing Company Ltd

Warner Books
A Division of
Little, Brown and Company (UK)
Brettenham House
Lancaster Place
London WC2E 7EN

This book is dedicated to all the little Rurus
out there in the middle of nowhere.
Hold on to your dream.

Special thanks to
Fenton Bailey,
Randy Barbato,
Renetta Freeman,
Craig Nelson,
Alison Pollet,
Dick Richards,
and
Victor Weaver

Foreword

I wrote this book because I wanted to reveal my soul to the world.

I wanted to show the human being that lives inside of me, the human being that lives inside us all.

And I particularly wanted to do this because, as a drag queen, people generally see me as some kind of thing or freak with a sex fetish. I've never understood why people find it so hard to recognize the real person inside of me.

Drag for me is showtime. That's entertainment! I don't go shopping in a bra and panties, and I don't vacuum the apartment in high heels. So when I go to work, it's no different than a businessman wearing his three-piece suit on Wall Street. I'm like a nurse, a fireman, or a cop on the beat—they all wear their uniforms to work, and I'm no different. And, like all professionals, I love my uniform.

After all, whether we are at work or at play we are all wearing masks and playing roles all the time. Like I've always said, "You're born naked and the rest is drag."

But when I give out my job description, people always attach "Sex Fetish" to my career choice. No one ever thinks twice about the priest in his robe or the Supreme Court justice in his gown. And if you ever went up to a motorcycle cop and asked if he was into leather and domination, you would probably be arrested.

Whether we are in uniform or not, it's easy for people to label and categorize other people; in this way they make them small, trite, and ultimately inhuman.

But I will not be ignored. The soul that lives inside this body will not be ignored. I am here to stay.

And I am here to say that we are all gods and goddesses, each and every one of us.

With all humility, I think the universe is using me to express that message in a fun, colorful way—so that people can get it instantly and connect with it emotionally instead of having to think about it.

In this book I'm going to show you that I am just like everybody else. I hope when you are done reading this book, you'll put it down and say, "Oh my God! I've just read my own life story." That's what I mean by letting it all hang out.

One of the questions I am so often asked is, "What do I call you? He or she?" And I say, "You can call me he, you can call me she, you can call me Regis and Kathie Lee, just so long as you call me." It's important not to get caught up in formalities. Some people try to avoid calling me anything at all, as if they are afraid of something; is it drag queens that they are afraid of, or is it themselves?

Sometimes I think they see the reflection of themselves when they look into my eyes. . . . Most people are afraid of what lurks deep inside of themselves. They spend a lifetime running away from it or smothering it with food, sex, drugs, or alcohol. One of life's biggest challenges is to look in the mirror because there's really nothing to be afraid of.

Most men don't do femininity well, mostly because in our culture it's forbidden. But I think everyone—just once in their lives—should wear a dress, work a wig, and slip on some pumps!

It's always interesting to see someone transformed by the glamour of drag. You see an aspect of their personality that you would not otherwise see. To this point you've only seen half the story, now you're getting to see the other half: the flip side of the coin, the dark side of the moon. Now, for the first time, you can see the whole person, the god *and* the goddess inside of everyone. It's a revelation.

It's really no different from when the little boy puts on a cowboy outfit for the first time and starts acting big and tough like John Wayne. You see, clothes aren't just things you wear—they bring out the flavor of the person, magnifying hidden areas of your personality that spend most of the time cooped up in the cellar of your consciousness. From time to time you need to take them out for a walk around the block to stretch their legs.

I'm an old pro; I was doing Revlon commercials in my mother's bedroom at the age of eight. I got my first Barbie doll when I was five years old. The fact that I sawed her breasts off had more to do with that boyhood destructive thing than misogyny. Other than that slight hiccup, exploring my feminine side came very easily to me, because I grew up in a house full of women.

My immediate family, who were my role models and heroes, were all feminine. They were showing their emotions and wearing them in the same way they wore their clothes; when they were sad they cried, when something was funny they laughed out loud, and when something confused them they asked questions. I've always found strength in that, and comfort in my own femininity. I've always loved it, expressed it, lived it.

And that's why I do it so well, and why people react to it so well. I've never had to talk in a woman's voice or put on airs, I've always been myself. So it's never been this weird thing where people look at me and go, "That guy is trying to act like a woman." People are usually very comfortable with me in drag.

Because it was so natural to me it took me a long time to figure it out, but I can explain it like this: "The reality is that I am a man. The illusion is that I am a woman. But of the two, the illusion is truer."

But now that's changing too. Ironically, just as the world is getting to know me in my female extravaganza, I'm getting to know my own personal maleness.

Executive Realness, Spring 1994.

As I write this I am not wearing a wig, I am not wearing a pair of high heels, and I have *not* lost my mind. I'm looking gorgeous in Timberlands, oversize baggy pants worn down low, and a homeboy flannel shirt. Just as I have explored different female looks—black hooker, gender fuck, and supermodel—now I am exploring different drag male looks—J. Crew preppy, sexy homeboy, and executive realness.

Just as when I am in drag I feel totally at ease with my feminine side, now, for the first time in my life, I feel totally at ease with my masculine side. It's not just the way I look, it's the way I *feel* that I am projecting. In fact it has more to do with what's coming from the inside than things on the outside, like my goatee or my baggy pants. And I'm loving it! It's almost like I've found a long-lost twin brother and been reunited with something that, until now, was just a shadow in my life.

This is such a revelation to me in terms of my growth as a human being. And it's very much a part of my work. I want to present a whole and complete picture—the yin, the yang; the black, the white; the boy, the girl; the sane, the insane. Because we are all Everyman—a rainbow of different roles and different people.

Exploring the colors in myself and in others is my life's passion. There is no such thing as normality—each and every one of us, if we dare to be whole, is a gorgeous peacock.

Whether you believe we have one life to live or hundreds, there is no reason not to spread your wings and fly!

Chapter 1

How to Tuck

Going to work is not just a question of putting on some lip gloss and a little underarm deodorant. I don't care whether you're a high-class hooker, supermodel, or a tired old drag queen, every night is the big night. You have to look your best for your public, whatever you're selling. And I know what people expect of me—nothing less than perfection.

It's gonna take nothing short of a miracle for this to happen in just three short hours, and that's what a queen is —a miracle worker. The first thing I do is say a little prayer. I go to my vanity and pray to the gods of Charles Revson, Max Factor, Flori Roberts, and all the other patron saints of beauty. Then I run a hot bubble bath with gorgeous bath oils from Origins—because I'm a nat- ural queen. I unplug the phone, light some incense (Jasmine Extravaganza), and select the music that I will be listening to: something by Diana Ross, Donna Summer, or Barbra Streisand. This particular night I will be

listening to Cher's *Greatest Hits,* which includes "Save Up All Your Tears," my fave Cher song of all time. It has become the theme song for my transformation. All that pain and suf-

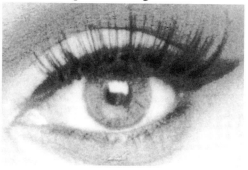

fering for great beauty. It hurts, but you mustn't grumble and mustn't cry—big girls don't cry.

After testing the temperature of the water with my toe, I tell my faithful intern Juan, "No matter what happens, or what you hear, do not open this door for the next three hours." Then I lock and double-bolt the door, and slowly begin to shed my manly disguise. I toss the clothes into a corner, where they watch discarded and miserable, unable to believe the transformation they are about to witness as the Goddess is born. I slip into the tub and before I move another muscle I soak for a good fifteen minutes. Then, very slowly, I take my loofah sponge and scrub my skin. The skin must be clean and supple, with every pore exfoli- ated, every dead skin cell removed before I can begin the process of shaving.

I start by putting lather on my head, my face, my beard, mustache, and neck. I shave with disposable razors and shaving gel. I shave my face closely so that if by chance that evening a fan should brush a hand against my cheek, they'll feel the silky smoothness of a baby's bottom. I used to shave upwards but no longer recommend this because it irritates the skin. I also shave my head so it's a chrome dome. Having had a mohawk for years as a teenag- er, I'm a virtuoso with the disposable razor. I go in a row like a farmer with his crops, from the front to the back, from my sideburns to the nape of my neck. Then I stand up in the tub and put the lather on my chest, stomach, and bikini line and shave it all off. At this point I'm shaving downwards to avoid the curse of ingrown hairs. Then I shave under my arms, and my legs. If the Goddess is required to reveal herself at a photo session, I'll also shave my arms, my fingers, and even the hair on my toes. The last to go are my eyebrows. Once that's done I'm like an artist's canvas, ready to beat my face into a masterpiece worthy of hanging in the Louvre. Paris, France, baby.

By now the water is good and funky, so I get out of the tub, rinse off in the shower, and immediately moisturize my whole body. I cannot stress enough the importance of this next step. This is something my mother told me from the time I was ten years old. She said, "Ru, moisturize, moisturize, moisturize." I use any type of lotion. I don't believe in paying more than ten bucks for a bottle of moisturizer, because a cheap queen can still be a beauty queen.

Before beginning on my face I do some odds and ends; check my face and reshave any telltale stubble so that my skin is smooth as marble. Then I put on deodorant—one that is strong enough for a man, but made for a woman. I floss and brush my teeth for a minimum of two minutes, light another stick of incense, and let my body relax for a minute. I have found in the past that if you bum rush the transformation, you get a less than stellar result. Breathing, relaxing, being calm—this is half of what it's all about. The transformation is both physical and mental. The Goddess is as much a state of mind as a look.

Then I slip into my blue and white robe that I "borrowed" from a hotel in Japan to start on my makeup. The robe is necessary because I don't want to get makeup powder all over my shoulders which will, in turn, rub off on the couture gowns I will be wearing that evening. I sit myself down in front of my mirror and line up all the tools I will be using to create this living work of art.

My mirror is brightly lit because I only use 100-watt bare bulbs. Now I know that nothing is more vulgar than a bare bulb, but I won't have anything else in my bathroom.

If you're a performer whose gonna have your picture taken, you *have* to make yourself up in the brightest light possible, because often your beard stubble can shine through the flash of a camera and cause unsightly discoloration. When I'm on the road I find that a lot of hotel lighting is really bad for makeup, so you have to carry your own light show. To get the features and the shadows right, you need the light coming at you from the top of the mirror and just above your head.

I start by putting some lip balm on my lips, and perhaps a little more moisturizer on my face. Then, I put on my foundation. Now you wouldn't build a building without a good foundation, and I am here to tell you that it is no different with constructing a face. The foundation must be solid. This is the biggest problem I have with makeup artists who are not drag queens—they don't slap that stuff on thick enough. If you have a makeup artist who's only used to doing real girls, it just doesn't work. Most real girls don't have a beard. I also have a face full of freckles, and even though I love Sissy Spacek, I am not featuring her. That's why I love Mathu—my stylist and makeup fave—because he understands these things. The foundation I use is Mac Studio Makeup N7. Not only does it give me the full coverage I need, it is totally cruelty-free and has *not* been tested on animals—other than men. First I apply it all over my face, sparingly and evenly, and then I go back over it with a spatula and plaster it on like stucco. It's important to use expensive sponges because they don't crumble.

While the makeup is still wet, I take Mac Studio Makeup N3, which is the same tone as my base but lighter, and highlight the areas that I want to bring forward; under my eyes, out to my cheekbones, the bridge of my nose, and up into my forehead. I'll put some light on the top inner socket of my eyes and a dab of light on my chin. These are the points that the light will hit and it will make them come forward.

Then I take Mac Studio Makeup N10, which is the same tone as my base but darker, and put it under my neck, right under my cheekbones, and above my temples on the side of my forehead. I contour my nose by putting some dark on either side, which both straightens and thins it—à la Michael Jackson.

What I'm doing with these combinations of shadows and light is sculpting my face, bringing out the cheekbones and minimizing the masculine parts of my face. If I'm wearing a low-cut outfit I'll also put makeup on my chest. I will contour that so it's darker in the center of my chest, lighter where the tits are, so that when I put my push-up bra on it looks like real cleavage. And it does. I blend all that in so it's a nice even tone, and looks somewhat natural. But natural ain't got nothing to do with it.

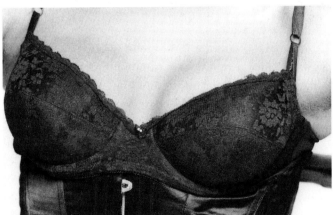

The last thing I do before I fix the whole beautiful creation with powder is shape my eyes. I'll do my eyebrows in the dark brown pancake. I'm not very good at doing eyebrows, so if I make a mistake I can wipe them off, reapply the makeup, and start again. If I did this after I had powdered, I would be up the creek, past the point of no return. It's difficult to get the right line, because you have to see your face the way a makeup artist would see it, from slightly above and about three feet away. Now that is not an effect you are going to get by looking in the mirror, so it's guesswork. But if the eye-brows don't fit your face, if the curve isn't quite right, the rest is use-less—unless you're going  for the look of a snaggle-toothed hag, which is a look that I have found useful in the past. Once all the shading's done and I've got my eyebrows perfect, I take my translucent powder, which has a touch of tawny or caramel in it (my natural color), and powder the whole face to matte it. For an added touch I'll take a little white powder and brush it up over my cheekbone and under my eye, for a little more accentuation.

Then I start on my eyes. I take some light vanilla eye shadow and put it over the inside of my inner lid, and close to the nose on the outer brow. Then I take a light brown shadow and put it in the outer creases of my eyes—not in toward my nose, but out toward my temples. I blend that nicely, but not too much. With some dark brown I'll go over my eyebrows again. I'll curl my eyelashes—my real nat-ural eyelashes—and mascara them. Next I'll apply some liquid eyeliner on the top lids. Then I'll put the false eye-lashes on the top lids only. I use dark tone eyelash adhe-sive, because it dries black. I use orange mango matte blush for my cheeks plus a little bit on my forehead, and perhaps if I am feeling perky, some on my chin.

The lips are next. First I look in the mirror and say "I have beautiful lips." Then I take a brown eyebrow pencil and "perfect" the lip line, improving on nature's own handi-work by going a little bit over the top, because my top lip tends to disappear when I smile. Then I apply my lipstick. My lips are higher on the left than on the right, so with a lip brush I even them out. I'll even put another, lighter color

How to Tuck

on the inner bottom lip, so
that it pouts more.

With the lips done I
can begin to see the big picture—the glamourous con-
coction that will soon make
dogs bark in the street, birds
sing arias, and traffic
screech to a halt. All the
time I'm thinking about
how gorgeous I'm gonna
look, how this is all gonna
be worth it, because in drag
you feel like a superstar.
You get addicted to the
attention. There are times
when I haven't been in drag
for a long time and I really
begin to miss it, and long to
be a vision of foxiness
again.

At the same time I'm
also thinking about how
long I'm going to have to
keep it all on for, and how
long it can hold up under
the baking stagelights and
the glare of public scrutiny
before, like a melting
Polaroid, the whole vision
collapses.

Just as every sentence
needs a period at the end of
it, so every face is enhanced
by a beauty mark—it is
almost like the artist's sig-
nature, and it is always the
last thing I do.

Then I start getting

THINGS YOU NEED TO BE A DRAG QUEEN

1. Flawless, fierce attitude
2. Disposable razors
3. Shaving gel
4. Body lotion
5. Full coverage pancake makeup in light, medium, and dark
6. Translucent loose powder, plus a compact for your purse
7. Makeup sponges that don't crumble
8. Powder puff pads
9. Mango blush
10. Brown, black, and vanilla eye shadow
11. Black mascara
12. Eyelash curler
13. Black false eyelashes
14. Black and brown eyebrow pencils
15. Lipsticks: red, blackberry, and purple
16. Tweezers
17. Makeup applicators and brushes
18. Black cake eyeliner (add water)
19. Dark-toned false eyelash adhesive
20. Lip liner brush
21. Tucking panties
22. Panty hose
23. Corset
24. Push-up bra
25. Gym socks rolled up tight (for breasts)
26. High-heeled shoes
27. Hotpants, mini-dress
28. Gloves
29. Clip-on earrings and assorted jewelry
30. Press-on nails
31. Wigs
32. Perfume (I recommend "Whore"—for she who is)
33. Cocktail purse
34. A lot of time to get dressed
35. Positive love energy

dressed. In a swift single move I rip off my robe, and I'm totally naked as I rummage around my apartment for my corset and push-up bra. Half the thing about getting dressed the next day is finding where everything went as it flew off my body the night before. By the time I get in after a big night of glamour, my corset is cutting me in half. It's killing me! So I tear off all my clothes and rip that corset off faster than you can say, "Honey I shrunk the kids."

Taking a fresh pair of tucking panties from my linen closet, I begin that time-honored ritual known as "tucking." Tucking is a delicate procedure that I have described as an ancient Chinese secret. On other occasions I have said that I am "sitting on a secret," and that's really it in a nutshell. This is what you do; you put your tucking panties on. There are different types of tucking panties, such as specially made things called "gaffs," but I prefer to use girl's bikini bottoms. Mine are size small and made out of very-tight-woven Spandex. Then you take your penis (preferably your nonerect penis), and pull it back toward your butthole, pushing everything—balls and all—backward. In this way the front part of your pelvis is flat and your balls are between your legs, bisected by your penis, which is headed south toward the border. The penis lifts and separates the two contenders so that you have one testicle on either side delicately nestled like eggs between your thighs. It's important not to get a hard-on as you begin the process. From this point on put all thought of romance or sex out of your head. If you get aroused, all hell could break loose.

Then you adjust the fierceness of the tuck by pulling your panties up between your butt-cheeks in the back. Once in place, the panties will keep the whole package securely wrapped and bonded. I've been told that I have the fiercest tuck this side of the Mason-Dixon line, and I have the scars from the panties to prove it. Generally, as long as the tuck isn't too tight, it doesn't really hurt. But one wrong move can have the effect of a nutcracker and make the strongest of drag queens shriek, "Girl, call me a cab."

Then you put on your panty hose. I wear Woolworth's

own brand, Cameo, tall, sheer-to-waist. Now this can also be tricky. Since they are only the second thing you put on, you have to be very careful not to get a run. So many times I've gotten a run in my hose just as I'm running out the door—late! They've sent monkeys to the moon, *why* can't they invent panty hose that don't run? What is the problem here?

If I'm wearing support hose, getting a run is a moot point. If I'm wearing a bathing suit, I often wear opaque skin-tone support hose, because while I want to look naked, I don't want to feel it. Aerobic instructors on TV love this stuff. If you don't have support hose, my tip is to wear two or three pairs of panty hose—and they'll give you that secure, opaque feel.

Now it's time for the corset or waist cincher— although I prefer the former. For this I call in Juan, who's glad to return from exile. The corset is hooked in the front and tied in the back, and it gives you a tighter feel than a waist cincher. You hook up the latches on the front, and then you tighten it like tying a pair of shoes in the back. You pull, and you pull, and you pull until you get the desired effect—which is, ideally, a total inability to breathe. In the interests of survival, though, I normally compromise and tie the knot while I can still breathe, barely.

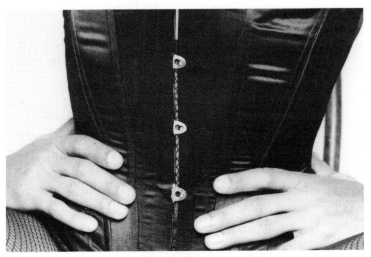

Next I slip into my nude bodysuit. My nude bodysuit

is designed to give the effect of being nude underneath, no matter what I am wearing. It's rather
like a flesh-colored bathing suit. Made specially for me, it
has different strap arrangements—strapless, criss-cross, or
spaghetti straps—and can accommodate any couture outfit.
It also has built-in titties.

At this point in the game I look like an exotic alien
from *Star Trek*. I am in hose, corsetry, and body suit, but
basically still butt naked. My head is also totally shaved.
But apart from that I am now, basically, womana.

Not only am I ready, but I am panting for the luxuri-
ous embrace of glamour. Tonight I will be wearing a gorgeous Todd Oldham creation. Once the dress is on, I go to
put my hair on. *Never* put the dress on after the wig. Wigs
are more than a piece of hair. A cat without its coat would
look pretty freaky, and a peacock without its feathers would
look downright ugly. A wig is like your fur—it's your second skin. So the wig is crucial, and to look remotely cred-
ible it needs to soften the harshness of a man's face. I wear
lace-front wigs, which are *very* expensive. But I'm worth
it. Now, lace-front wigs have a transparent mesh that is like
netting. It's invisible to the eye, and once it's on you cannot see the line. To secure it you put a little glue near the
sideburns of your head—although for the glue to stick you
have to take off the makeup from those areas first.

The hair has been designed, styled, and delivered prior

to this evening by top stylists. I have a special hatbox that carries the head and hair of RuPaul. It's actually a kick drum carrying case, lined with foam, with a mannequin head bolted in the middle. Most of my wigs will fit in this with room to spare. Once the wig has been styled, set with hair spray, and stashed in my box, you could play basketball with it. As you can imagine, some wig creations exceed carry-on hand luggage dimensions. Rather than face any hassles, I prefer to check my hair and forget all about it—something I feel comfortable doing with my specially built box.

After the wig it's shoe time, and kids, shoes are not to be taken lightly, especially when you have a size-thirteen pair of apple turnovers like I do. Shoes can either make or break the illusion—and if they are not the right size, they can break your feet as well. There is nothing more unsightly than a wobbling supermodel. You have to glide down the catwalk. The proper way to strut your stuff has nothing to do with your feet, it's all in your head. If you believe you can walk on air, you will walk on air, and walk on air I do in shoes from Frederick's of Hollywood. I buy in bulk, because after one or two wears there's nothing left. My favorites are nude mules because the strap over the toes is clear plastic, and that accentuates the legs, allowing them to taper off without interruption. I was there just after the L.A. riots and all the size thirteens had been looted. There must be a lot of gangsta queens prancing around the City of Angels.

But I don't have time to think about that now, because I'm late. The limousine is purring downstairs, and everything else that needs to be done happens real fast: shoes, jewelry, and gloves all go on simultaneously in the wink of an eye. As I fly out the door, the last thing I do is give myself a quick spritz of my perfume, Whore—*I created it for she who is.* Forget Poison, Passion, Free Willy, and all the other two-bit perfumes flooding the market. Whore is the ultimate when it comes to fragrant jewels, and, unlike all those others, Whore hits the spot. It takes a licking and keeps on ticking. Just one squirt and it has grown men barking like dogs.

On the ride uptown I have time to catch my breath, make a few final adjustments, and savor the moment. I know that as I step out of the stretch at the premiere, careful not to squish my updo, the paparazzi will go crazy. In that blinding orgasm of a thousand flashbulbs, all the effort, all the pain, and all the plucking will have been worth it. Knowing the pleasure that my fans will get from the photograph of me in tomorrow's *Women's Wear Daily,* looking flawless and gorgeous, makes me wanna cry real tears.

Are you ready for me?

Chapter 2

Little Ruru

I was born RuPaul Andre Charles.

Recently, I was talking to my cousin who told me the story of when my mother proclaimed me a star.

"Hey, Toni," Aunt Enorris yelled, "what you gonna call the baby?"

"His name is RuPaul Andre Charles," my mother replied. "And he's gonna be famous, 'cos ain't another motherfucker alive with a name like that."

And if you knew my mother, that's exactly what

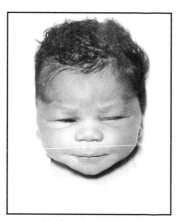

My first photo session. I worked the camera even at thirty minutes old.

she said, 'cause she had a mouth like a sailor.

My mother kept a copy of *Ebony* magazine from July 1960. The cover story was on Fats Domino, and inside there was a photo spread of him and his friends hanging out by the bar in the living room of his mansion. One of the friends in the picture was called Ripoll Roberts, and my mother had drawn an arrow pointing to his name with "Boy" written alongside it.

Both my parents were poor country folk from Louisiana, way out in the boondocks. They met in Beaumont, Texas, on a blind date. My dad, Irving Charles, was in the army and served in the Korean War. They married in Houston, Texas, where my mother gave birth to my twin sisters. Later they moved to San Diego during the great western migration, like so many other blacks from the South. My father was working as an electrician for McDonnell Douglas, the aircraft manufacturer, when I was born.

From left to right: Uncle Willie, Uncle Caffrey, Renetta, Pat, my mother holding me, Renae, and Margaret.

Our house was a California tract home in a modern development called Michelle Manor. It was a yellow three-bedroom house with a patio, which my father built in the back, and one-and-a-half bathrooms (one bathroom didn't have a tub in it). There was a two-car garage, a kitchen, living room, front yard, and a backyard with a big palm tree and lots of foliage. There were only four house prototypes within the develop-ment, so every fourth house was identical. The house across the street was exactly the same as ours. But no baby drag queens lived there.

So much has happened in that house. I can tell you a story for every nick in the wall. You name it, every-thing about that house is written on the walls. Take the burn mark above the dirty clothes hamper in the bathroom; at age thirteen, I used to sit on the toilet and practice smoking with my mother's Tarryton cig-arettes. One day I placed a cigarette on the hamper while plucking my eyebrows. The next thing I knew the cigarette had fallen into the hamper and started a fire. Luckily, I did not panic, but grabbed the shower head and doused the flames before they burned the whole house down and everything in it.

Then there's the nick in

Little Ruru goes to kinder-garten, four years old.

the bedroom wall where my sister Rozy tried to hit me with a hammer. I ducked. She swung, and hit the wall. Afterward I just laughed—that pissed her off even more.

But my favorite mark has to be the handprint above the light switch in the kitchen. One summer's day my sisters and I were all hanging in the kitchen when my mother came home from work. She walked in the door and as usual started telling every-body what to do: "Renae, get off your high-yellow ass and go get the clothes off the clothesline." Renae rolled her eyes and sucked air through her teeth. Mama caught this out of the corner of her eye and went to give Renae a backhand slap. Renae instinctively jumped out of the way and Mama's hand slammed into the wall, leaving a print and a crack. We all busted out laughing as Mama jumped around the house screaming every curse word imaginable.

My memory suggests—and research corroborates this—that I wasn't a mean or bratty little boy. I was a good baby. You could just sit me in the corner and I would be fine—no screaming, just content. My sister Rozy, on the other hand, needed lots of attention. If you sat *her* in the corner, she would start crying and you'd have to say, "Come on, it's okay." Rozy and I fought with each other a lot. At breakfast we would put the cereal box in front of each other's faces so we wouldn't have to see one another. Then we would fight over who got to read the back of the box first. Captain Crunch was our favorite. Apart from my spats with Rozy, I was very sweet and sensitive.

My neighbors were kind and generous, and often they would take me under their wings. I would go over to my neighbor Stark's house, where they would fix me breakfast. Stark was about twenty-five, a big, burly black man who was in the navy. He lived with his girlfriend, Billie, and her three children. He used to yell out to me in the morning, "Ruru, come on over here and have some scrambled eggs. They'll put hair on your chest!" He never struck me as the kind of man you said no to, so I always took him up on his offer—not realizing then how problematic a hairy chest might be for certain career choices.

First grade, five years old.

Another of my earliest memories was sitting on my father's shoulders watching television. I liked to lick the top of his bald head because it was salty. I remember the commercials from back then more than the actual television shows. I used to love Edie Adams doing those Tiparillo cigar commercials. She would do big Broadway-style production numbers in gorgeous evening gowns, dripping with fur, and surrounded by male dancers. The commercial would always end with her saying, "Why don't you come up and see me sometime?" I had no idea that she had stolen the line from Mae West, but I loved it all the same. At the other end of the scale was the commercial for Dutch Master cigars, with thirteen old Dutchmen standing around in black Pilgrim outfits and huge white collars. Those guys scared me to death.

Me in the second grade. My teacher said I daydreamed too much..

I remember telling my mother once "Mama, from now on call me 'Education,' 'cause I'm gon get me a education." I knew all along that she loved hearing that and still remember her leaning out of the front door and yelling, *"Education, education, education"* when it was time to come in for supper. That was our little joke. It was rather ironic since I was never very good in school. I always tried to do well and be the teacher's pet, but they never picked me. Instead, my teachers would send me home with notes complaining about the fact that I was forever looking out of the window and daydreaming. My second-grade teacher wrote a report card that said: "RuPaul looks out of the window too much. He needs to focus on what's going on *inside* the class." Forget about it! To this day, if there's an open window, I can just gaze out and leave the planet. I'm like a big balloon, and unless I'm careful to keep myself on the ground, I just drift right off into outer space. The teachers said that if only I applied myself, I could be quite good. Eventually, I took that advice—not in terms of being good at the homework, but in terms of applying myself.

After school I would hook up with my friends

and we would all hang out in the Canyon. For a while Albert was my best friend and we had a big thing building go-carts by stealing the wheels off shopping carts and nailing them to two-by-fours stolen from the development being built up the street. We had a tree house in the Canyon and we would go there and smoke cigarettes. I wasn't a saint, but at least I wasn't carjacking or getting fucked up— yet.

At some point all gay children realize that they are different, out of sync or set apart from what everyone else is doing. I think this often happens sooner rather than later—years before you have any idea what sex is or who Liza Minnelli is. I have a memory of me at five years old, lying in the fetal position in the hallway of my house. I remember looking down at myself, so it must've been an out-of-body experience,

and I was thinking to myself, "I'm insane, I'm crazy." Even then I knew I had a different perspective on the world. I was not doing the same things other kids were doing, and I was looking at things as an observer, as an outsider, like an alien.

For example, I always wondered why people didn't say, "Okay, everyone, just stop! Do you feel insecure? Do you feel like you're not worth crap?" If people only did that the answer would be, "Why yes, I do feel those things. Let's talk this through." Why, I wondered, did we just carry on ignoring our feelings, pretending that they didn't exist? Why didn't we take the time out to do something about them, so we didn't have to feel that way anymore? I just could not shake the sensation that I didn't belong, and that this was not my real home. You know what? It isn't. Planet Earth

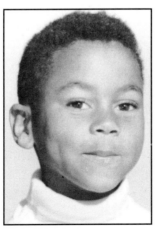

Me at eight years old in the third grade.

is a high school from hell, and we are all just students here. When I realized that, I screamed out loud. I've always felt like a foreign exchange student, a resident alien. You come here for one thing and one thing only, and that is to learn. I used to spend a lot of my life waiting for the day I could quit school, but then I came to realize that so long as we are alive we never leave school. Life is a series of high schools, one after the other. And if you don't study, do your homework, and learn enough in one lifetime, you just get sent back and have to do it all over again.

Because I was always so sensitive, I'd often get my feelings hurt, and would cry easily. Mama would say something to me—she could be very harsh—and I would go and cry. Other times I got upset by kids or my older sisters teasing me. Even when I was really young, kids would come up to me and say, "You should have been a girl, and your sister Rozy should have been a boy." Before I knew anything about my sexuality, people would say, "You're a sissy," and I'd say, "What?" They weren't shy about saying the same thing twice. "You are a sissy," they'd say, and I would cry even though I had no idea what they were implying. "You're too sensitive, too sentimental" Mama would say.

And of course the whole boy/girl thing *was* an issue because I felt like neither one nor the other, and looked like something altogether different. When Christine Jorgenson, the first sex change, got her operation my sister Renetta cut out an article about it and gave it to me. I said, "Why are you giving me this?" She said, "Oh, you should read about this." "Hmmm," I thought to myself.

Generally, I did wonder what the deal was; why was I so different from the other boys, and why was it so difficult for me to blend in? I loved being around girls because they were free to express themselves emotionally, and I have always felt that emotions are what being a human is all about. Boys, on the other hand, were blind to their emotions. They denied their feelings by acting or lying, and I couldn't understand why they would do that. There were times when I thought there must have been a mistake, that

RuPAUL'S FAVORITE SAYINGS

1. Don't let your mouth write a check your ass can't cash.
2. Don't let the smooth taste fool ya.
3. Your country breakfast is ready.
4. You got some money for me?
5. Strong enough for a man, made for a woman.
6. If I'm lying I'm flying, and you don't see no wings, do ya?
7. You better work, bitch . . .
8. Everybody say love.
9. She done already done had hers'es.
10. If you don't love yourself, how in the hell you gonna love somebody else?
11. All right, god damn it!

maybe I *was* a girl stuck in a boy's body. But, after puberty, I was quite happy being a boy. I have always felt quite straightforward and uncomplicated about being a man who likes other men.

When I was ten, I tongue-kissed Tiny, the girl across the street. I also took her panties off—mainly because I wanted them for myself! I may have even touched her kooter. Everybody teased us and said, "Oh look, they're boyfriend and girlfriend." I went along with it, and would say, "Yeah, me and Tiny across the street, we're boyfriend and girlfriend." Then, when I was thirteen, I tongue-kissed a girl named Queen Esther, and that was the extent of my romances with the opposite sex.

It wasn't really an unhappy childhood—but it wasn't a fairy tale either. When we were little kids, my parents would fight all the time, real fistfights. Renae, Renetta, Rozy, and me would huddle together in the back while they battled with one another in the front room, screaming at each other and tearing the place apart. By the time we came out of hiding in the morning, everything was all over the place; bits of shattered lamps, broken plates, and glasses everywhere. It was a total mess.

It was like something straight out of *The Prince of Tides.* In the movie the kids went underwater when their parents started fighting because it was peaceful there, a safe haven. When I saw that film I started crying uncontrollably, and not silently. It was embarrassing because I literally could not control myself. The movie triggered these feelings that just gushed out of me. As children we bury a lot of our feelings deep inside and learn to become experts at hiding our emotions behind masks. Much later in life some catalyst, some event, will bring them all back, and they will all pour out, even stuff we forgot was there. So there I was in a theater full of people, gasping for breath—I couldn't stop it.

I remember the day my childhood ended very clearly. It was the day my parents went to file for their divorce. Normally, I would come home for lunch every day, and my mother would be there with oatmeal or something. But that particular day, I went home for lunch and no one was there. So I went back to school, lined up ready to go back into class, and suddenly started crying. My teacher asked me what was wrong and I explained that I had gone home to lunch but my mother wasn't there, and so I hadn't had anything to eat. She sent me off with a note to the cafeteria. As I trotted off I felt better already because of this special treatment. I was on an adventure! When I got there the cafeteria was totally empty except for the janitors who were cleaning off tables. They only had some hot dogs and potato chips left, but I didn't mind. A few minutes later as I sat eating my lunch, the principal came over and said, "May I join you?" I nodded, and the two of us proceeded to eat lunch together. It was my first power meal. After all, having lunch with the principal was like having lunch with the President of the United States. I can still remember the rush of being with a VIP, and not feeling so stranded after all.

Chapter 3

Mean Miss Charles

My mother at fourteen.

My mother was Creole and came from St. Martinsville, Louisiana. It's near where they make Tabasco. But my mother was the hottest bottle of sauce for miles around—a real firecracker of a woman.

My mother was mulatto. It's a weird color—I can never quite describe it—neither black nor white but something else, a sort of beige. She had six brothers and sisters, two of them died at birth, and the surviving brothers and sisters—Frank, Felicia, Mandolia, Enorris—moved to California in the fifties. My grandparents' names were Ernestine Gerard and Felix Fontinette. My mother was named Ernestine Fontinette after her mother, and she was every bit as bold and grand as her name suggests. When my mother was fifteen, her mother was mad at her for something and said to her, "You make me so mad sometimes, I wish I hadn't given you my name!" My mother said, "Fine! I'll change my name!" And from then on she had everyone call her Toni, which is what my dad called her. The social workers called her Mrs. Ernestine Charles. All the kids in the neighborhood called her Mean Miss Charles.

Mama was full of one-liners. She was wise in many ways, but dysfunctional in others. Still, some of her words of wisdom were hard to forget, like, "Never argue with a fool." I go by that to this day. There's no point to it. Another one was, "Blind Tom said, 'Sight beat the world, and we shall see.'" As a child I had no idea what this meant, and I only recently figured it out. It basically means the truth will make itself known.

My mother was very clean. She wasn't a clean freak like Joan Crawford, but she liked to keep her house clean. Another one of Mama's bits of advice was, "If you don't have nothing to your name, at least keep it clean." That was her philosophy. I was a boy, so I got away with keeping my room a mess. It's funny how ulti-

Mean Miss Charles.

mately you turn into your parents. If you go to my house today, it's not spick and span—I may throw my corset on the floor— but it is clean, especially the bathroom and the kitchen.

Toni at twenty-three partying with friends.

I have an early memory of my mother walking me to kindergarten. It was a sunny day, and I cried when she left me there. But the thing I remember most of all was the dress she had on. It was very sixties, very op art, with big brown circles in black squares against a beige background, the sort of thing you see in old curtains, mostly. It was cut so that it flowed out at the waist and went below the knee. My mother was a fashion plate. Next to her idol Jackie O. she was best the dressed woman in the United States. Simple but elegant.

Around the house her hair was all messy and she only wore a caftan, and I have that caftan to this day, as well as her collection of costume jewelry, which she used to collect with a passion. Since she knew what her son would need for a full and happy life, she left it to me in her will. Mama's passion for shopping turned me into someone who doesn't like to shop. She would drag us around with her shopping all day with her friend Phyllis from up the hill saying, "Should I get this?" or, "What do you think of that?"

By the time I was seven, my mother and father had had enough of each other, and my father moved out. I don't remember them ever being in love or even together—there was always tension between them, and so in a way we were glad once he was gone, because we knew he had made my mother unhappy.

Now, my mother would have you believe that she kicked Daddy out, but no one can be kicked out of their own house. That was just the way my mother was; "I'm a bold, black bitch" was her favorite line. She was really in love with him in a big way, and, I guess, in the wrong way. I remember standing across the street from our house when I was about six with the whole neighborhood watching my parents in the garage. My mother had poured gasoline all over my father's car and was holding a book of matches in her hand and screaming, "Motherfucker, I will light this! I will ignite this motherfucker!" Meanwhile, my dad was on the other side of the car saying, "Toni—don't do it. Stop!" Sister Harris from my mother's church came and talked her out of doing it. The fire department was there too, and crowds all around. I didn't realize it at the time, but if she had done that she would have killed herself, killed him, and burned the house down, with us kids watching from across the street. Very Movie of the Week. My mother was very much that way; Leo the lion, born July 24, 1927. That French, Napoleonic-type thing. Hot temper. Very much so.

That particular episode was triggered by the affair my dad was having with someone else. Betty—that was the other woman's name. It broke my mother's heart. By that time they were already sleeping in separate rooms, but when she found out about it she went in and spray-painted Betty's name all over the yellow walls in red while he was out. All over. In fact she did such a good job that even though the room has been painted dozens of times since, there are still traces of that red paint there today.

My parents divorced in 1967, and my mom never really recovered from it. After the divorce she literally had a nervous breakdown. One day she just stayed in bed and stopped functioning completely. That was the day my two older sisters Renae and Renetta became adults, because they had to become parents looking after me, my sister, and my mother, who continued to stay in bed for days. My mother also started seeing a psychiatrist. His solution to her problems was an endless supply of Librium and

Valium. This was the beginning of some pretty scary times. Because of the drugs, you never knew what kind of mood she'd be in. So you would approach her very tentatively, like, "Ma, can I have a quarter for some pop?" And she would either say, "Yeah, Ru baby, just look in my purse and get what you want," or else she'd scream, "YOU PUSSY-MOUTHED MOTHERFUCKER GET YOUR BLACK ASS OUT OF MY FACE!"

Matters weren't helped by the fact that she didn't get along with my father's side of the family—even when they were married. She maintained that they never liked her because she was light-skinned and they were all dark-skinned. They thought she thought that she was too good for them. She was always aloof and her own person, so she certainly didn't make things any easier. To a certain extent they were projecting their own insecurities onto her, but then, for her part, she actually did think she was too good for them. Especially after a party at my father's sister's house for which my mother had her friend Hilda make a beautiful satin dress with pearls on it. It was really gorgeous, and before she went she was so excited because she was gonna be the best dressed there. The first night—it was a long weekend party—some of the guests slept over at the house. But when my mom woke up in the morning, she saw that the dress she was going to wear had been slashed to bits with razor blades. In her room! While she slept! She never found out who did it, but that was the last straw, although as far as the party went she played it cool and wore something else.

That was the last time she took any shit from them. In fact, from then on she handed it out. One afternoon after the divorce, one of my father's sisters came round to check up on us kids. My mom had just gotten in and was hanging up her coat when she answered the door.

"What the hell you want?" Mama said.

"Irving wanted me to come over and see what's going on with Renae," said my aunt.

"It ain't any none of your goddamned business," said my mother.

With that my aunt tried to push her way into the house.

Big mistake!

My mother had a wire hanger in her hand and started beating her with it. Somehow it got caught on her nose and ripped it wide open. There was blood everywhere! Fortunately, my aunt's daughter was with her, and rushed her to the hospital, where she had eighteen stitches. Next morning the front porch looked like something out of *The Texas Chainsaw Massacre*. Needless to say, my aunt didn't come round much more after that.

Although everyone used to call her Mean Miss Charles, I didn't think she was that mean, and in fact it wasn't till I got older that I learned that other parents didn't say things like, "Get your black ass in here, you little pussy-mouthed motherfucker, or I'll whip your goddamn ass." That was one of her famous ones—"pussy-mouthed moth-erfucker"—I think she must have coined it. My mother was a poet when it came to cussing someone out. She came from a long line of cussers and was fluent in this whole other language that had its own rules, had its own grammar, and had its own rhythms. It wasn't just random obscenities, but time-honored tongue-lashings designed to reduce you to a stuttering mute. She swore the way Olivier delivered Hamlet. She would curl her lip, grit her teeth, squint her eyes, and deliver a one-two punch like Muhammad Ali.

She wouldn't let us have kids come over to the house at all. If kids did come over she would say to me (with the kids standing right there in front of her), "What did I tell you about having them little black motherfuckers in my house? You take your little nappy-headed friends some-place else!" And then later when the kids would ask me, "Why is your mother so mean?" I'd say, "She's not really that mean, she's a pussycat." But I didn't know other peo-ple didn't talk that way, that's just how I grew up.

She would never go to school plays or functions, even when the teachers sent us home with notes asking our par-ents to come. She would just say, "You tell them teachers to come round here and kiss my black ass." Other times we

1. I don't lend, I don't borrow, and I don't visit.
2. Blind Tom said, "Sight beat the world and we shall see."
3. Ain't no two ways about it.
4. Repetit and Gone.
5. You think I'm drinking water through my ass?
6. A fool and his money soon part.
7. Don't let the same snake bite you twice.
8. What comes around goes around.
9. Don't take my kindness for weakness.
10. You can lead a horse to water, but you can't make him drink.
11. Still waters run deep.
12. A circle always meets.
13. I'd rather drink muddy water than sleep in a hollow log.
14. There's a time and a place for everything.
15. Pussymouthed motherfucker.

would be out with her at a grocery or department store, and she'd go after some poor store attendant and cuss them out. We would plead with her, beg her, not to start acting up. Often that would be enough to set her off, but at least it was us she went after rather than some innocent bystander. But if she didn't like you, she just didn't like you, and there was no two ways about it. She didn't pretend or anything like that. Still, her bark was worse than her bite. Meeting you for the first time she might say, "Motherfucker, what you lookin' at?" But if you could withstand that and hold your own, she'd be cool with you after that.

You can see why I really only wanted to please my mother—as all us kids did. There was a period when *Laugh-In* became the thing in 1969, and Mama said, "Okay, Ru, let's do it, do your thing." I would get up and do impersonations in the living room for my mother and my sisters. I would do Charo, Cher, Carol Burnett, Tina Turner, James Brown, and Elvis. I would also do the people across the street, because they had a thick southern black accent, particularly this man called Nate, who was one of our neighbors. My mother especially loved it when I did him, and pleasing her made me happiest of all.

Back then we were on welfare. They didn't have food stamps, but there was surplus cheese, butter, flour, and sugar that you could get. I remember going down to the welfare department to pick stuff up and the other kids would tease you chanting, "I can tell by ya knees ya eat commodity cheese!"

Mom used to sit at the kitchen table drinking coffee and looking out the window. From there you could see everything that was happening from our front porch all the way down the street. If a salesman, Jehovah's Witness, or social worker came to the door, she could see them coming. When they knocked on the door, she wouldn't answer it. Then they would back up, try and catch her eye through the window by waving or something, and then go back to the door and knock again. She still wouldn't answer it. This would go on until they got the message that she did not want to be bothered.

Sometimes she would make us answer the door. The social workers were the worst. They'd want to know everything that was going on: if there was a man living there, if our mother was working, if we were going to school, if our father was sending child support checks—which of course he wasn't. But we didn't say anything, we had been trained early on by my mother not to let any information leave the house. So we learned how to keep secrets at an early age, which is too bad, because kids shouldn't be keeping secrets.

Miss Charles in her favorite caftan watering the grass.

After her breakdown my mother had to build herself up from scratch. That took about three years, until 1970, when her father died. Suddenly she seemed to come into her own. She picked herself up and got a job with Planned Parenthood, where she worked until 1976. After that she got a job as a registrar, admitting students to San Diego City College. She made a decent living, paid off the mortgage, and supported herself.

My mother held a grudge against my father from the day they were divorced, and painted a picture of him in our minds as a no-good, dirty-rotten scoundrel. She also swore that my father and his sisters had put voodoo on her. Once she found a little Susie Homemaker doll in the front yard. Someone had painted stuff on its eyes and done other funky things to it too. From the day that the trouble started to the day she died, she always cursed his name and always, I mean always, had something bad to say about him. She was obsessed with the whole thing for twenty-five years, a quarter of a century—now that's a long time to hold a grudge. I've learned that this behavior is unhealthy. In fact it does the person holding the grudge more harm than it does the person against whom the grudge is held.

I think that's what killed her. She died of cancer. I truly believe that a lot of things like that, thoughts trapped inside the body, manifest themselves as physical ailments. So it's important to heal those thoughts by bringing them back up to the surface from the cellar of your heart where you've locked them away. By doing that you can change your perception of how things are, and let go of the old perception. And if you don't do that those thoughts can poison and kill you—body and soul.

Now, Mama kept it all inside and internalized everything. Altogether she was something of a closed book. I don't know very much about her at all. I always tried to get her to open up, but she never wanted to talk about her past or her people. In frustration I would go to my mother's bedroom, go through all her stuff, and read her letters. She would cuss me out for spying on her, but I wasn't really spying—I just wanted to know. Well, I never found out much. I've learned more from my cousins and my aunts than I have from her. I know that she had malaria as a child, that she'd gone to Catholic school, and was a practicing Seventh Day Adventist (although she didn't go to church because she thought it was a waste of time), and that's pretty much it. Very secretive. I put it down to that deep southern vibe. A lot of mysteries still linger there—

and my mother's just one of them.

Although she didn't tell me much about her past, I learned plenty from her. I learned how to stand up for myself. I learned how to break away from the pack, how to do my own thing and not let what other people thought of me get in the way. Above all, she was my ultimate inspiration because she was the first drag queen I ever saw. She had the strength of a man and the heart of a woman. She could be hard as nails, but also sweet and vulnerable—all the things we love about Bette Davis, Joan Crawford, and Diana Ross. To this day when I pull out my sassy persona, it's Ernestine Charles that I am channeling.

So even though she was a very remote, secretive, and not particularly affectionate person, I loved her very much. I was always close to her and passionate with her. Whenever I went to hug her she would say, "Get your hands off of me." But I would say, "Nope, nope, nope, hug, hug, hug!" and she'd just have to put up with it.

I think she liked it, really.

Chapter 4

School Daze

With Mama out at work all day, I really came into *my* own. I was free to let my hair down, quite literally. By age ten I was braiding and bleaching it. Mama would come home and say, "Nigger, you are crazy. Why'd you wanna do that?" I had a huge red Afro. My mother hated it, but she didn't make me cut it. At one point I took a tape measure to it, and it was seventeen inches deep. It was so big that it would flop in the middle, so I finally cut it.

I also smoked my first joint when I was ten. My friend Albert had stolen it from his brother, June Bug. We went up the street to the new tract home development they were building, where we sat on this box and smoked it. We giggled endlessly for about six straight hours, busting up about everything. We were in heaven. From that day on, I was hooked. But as a mere ten-year-old it was difficult to finance my pot smoking. I didn't know what to do. Then I came up with the idea of collecting cans and bottles for coin redemption. My sister and I would scour the neighborhood with a big plastic bag collecting them. The neighbors loved the fact that we were helping to clean up the neighborhood. "Such good little children," they'd say! Little did they know what we were spending it on.

Me at ten years old. My freckles made their world debut in the fifth grade.

We were terrors. We had a clubhouse in Albert's garage, where we would smoke our weed and listen to music. We used to have sleepouts in the backyard, go on stealing sprees at the drugstore, and hang out on the corner under the streetlight until one o'clock in the morning—all pretty innocent stuff. Sometimes we would sit in Renetta's old Ford, parked in my mother's front yard, and smoke pot. Sometimes we would steal the keys and take off driving. We almost wrecked the car, but it was a good way to learn how to drive.

Pose, Baby Ru, pose.

With pot I'd found what I needed to get through my horrible adolescence. Because I felt I was just biding my time, I needed something to placate me and help me tolerate my mundane existence. To me, at the time, San Diego was Nowheresville, so I would get stoned and daydream about moving to New York and becoming a star. In those days pot was a godsend. Of course, I don't feel that way

From left to right: Me, Rozy, and Anthony from next door building a go-cart.

anymore. Most of my teenage years and my twenties were spent stoned on pot, but I'm not interested in being stoned now. I want to be there for myself. Eventually I learned how to get high naturally without doing drugs, because the truth is that you have it all inside of you, all the highs and all the lows.

From kindergarten to sixth grade I was in the same school, Alphonso Horton Elementary. It was a block from my house. In seventh grade my mother said it was okay for me to go to children's theater at Balboa Park, and I started taking acting lessons there. I loved it *so* much I started taking drama in junior high too.

I was already quite popular at school because I was never anonymous. Everybody always knew who I was. I had a unique name, so in roll call it was always, "Who's RuPaul?" I also had freckles, which definitely made me different from most other kids in my school, and I was also very feminine looking. From being around girls all the time I acted feminine too, and was continually being mistaken for a girl. So, I already had something of a

In ninth grade I was voted best dancer and best Afro.

name for myself as an androgynous enigma.

When ninth grade rolled around I decided to make something of it. At school they had a thing called the Breakfast Club. For an hour in the morning the cafeteria was turned into a disco before classes started. For breakfast you could buy chocolate milk, donuts, and chips, and they cleared out the tables so you could dance. It was the perfect way to get the kids to school on time. At the time, the bump was really big, and everybody was bumping to death—double bumping, regular bumping, electric bumping, every kind of bumping. Now I knew I could bump, but there was a part of me that was reluctant to shine, to assume "the position"—I didn't want to draw attention to myself. So I used to sit on the sidelines and watch my classmates boogie down. But on the other hand, there was another part of me, a bigger part of me, that *did* want to assume the position, that did want the attention, and that's what gave me the nerve to join in. I decided to make my debut with a new dance from L.A. called the Crypt walk. Apart from myself and this girl called Michelle, no one knew how to do it. So one morning I grabbed her and said, "Let's dance!"

This was the first time I ever danced at the Breakfast Club. And everybody parted the way as we were doing it, and I could hear them all whispering, "Oh my God, they're doing that new dance called the Crypt walk!" Olivia New-ton John did it in her TV specials and in *Xanadu*. It's a very basic simple step, just like putting one foot behind the other, but at the time, coming out of the bump, it was revolutionary.

Me and Renetta in January 1971. She has always been my soul sister.

So that year I broke into the Breakfast Club scene, and went from being a freak to being a superfreak—and a popular one at that; I was voted Best Dancer of the year and Best Afro of the year. I look back on it now and realize—not to sound too grandiose about it—that I was just answering the call of the Universe, simply saying, "I accept my

Me and Rozy playing pool, 1973. My Afro got so big it would flop straight down the middle.

destiny!" Once you do that, your life can flow like a river.

After the ninth grade I went to Patrick Henry High School. It was an open campus and you could sit outside. I do not exaggerate when I say that I never went to one class while I was there. Annette Bening was going there too, and I suppose had I gone to class I might have met her, married her, and she'd be having my babies instead of Warren's! But, instead, for three months I smoked pot, ditched class, and went to lunch. Then one day on the bus the vice principal got on and said something to me and I gave him a piece of my mind. He checked my records, saw that I hadn't been to classes, and said, "You go back to where you come from."

The one thing I knew I could not do was go back to where I came from. I was fourteen years old, more awkward than ever, and feeling more like an alien than ever before. Where was my UFO to take me home? My only refuge was in bong hits and television, and I did lots of both. I was changing fast, and something had to give.

My sister Renetta would prove to be my salvation.

Chapter

Three Sisters

I grew up in a house that was all girls. Surprise! I have three sisters and we all have the same initials: Renetta Ann Charles, Renae Ann Charles, and Rosalind Annette Charles. I once asked my mother why she did that, and she said it was because we were all "Real Ass Crazies."

My mother and Renae were always up against each other. Rozy is the stubborn one, and Renetta was always my mother's favorite. Even though Renae and Renetta were the twins, Renetta was my soul sister—we really were the twins. Rozy who is a year younger than me taught me how to tie my shoes, but it was Renetta who taught me how to walk the runway, having been a graduate of the Barbizon school of modeling. She was so excited

Clockwise from top left: Renae, Renetta, me, and Rozy.

about having a baby brother. Once she was baby-sitting me while our parents were out and decided to give me a bath. After the bath I would not stop crying, no matter what she did. When my parents got home they realized that in putting me into the bath she had broken my arm! She was heartbroken and felt so bad. Every time my dad has a few drinks he brings up that time I was in the hospital, just three months old. His eyes well with tears as he tells how it broke his heart to see his little Bunjo—his nickname for me—laid up with a broken arm.

Then when I was four I saw Diana Ross and the Supremes singing "Baby Love" on the Ed Sullivan show. It wasn't their first time on, but my first time seeing them. It was love at first sight. I remember saying to myself, "There, that one there, the one in the middle, that's me!" I recognized her energy as my energy. She looked so happy, so radiantly happy to be there, and it just blew me away. She had it. She was the girl with something extra. The other two girls were lovely, but they did not have the effect that Diana had on me. Immediately afterwards I went out to the garage, scrunched my shoulders up, bared all of my teeth, and and started singing "Baby Love." All the time thinking to myself, "I love her! I love her!" I was in ecstasy. It was nothing short of a vision. My experience in seeing Diana was a landmark for me, in the same way that it was for many other people. I've heard tell that when Oprah saw her *she* said, "Colored girl on television! *Colored girl on television!*" What I knew right away, and at that precise moment, was that I wanted to be a big star. And as fate would have it, my mother went to see a psychic around that time who told her that I was going to be famous. From then on I knew what my mission in life was.

I always felt lucky having two older sisters. Being seven years older they were a world unto themselves and seemed to know so much about everything. In fact it was my twin sisters who turned me on to pop culture. They told me about Cybill Shepherd, who at that time was the big teen model for *Seventeen* magazine. She was everywhere. She was the Kodak / Noxema / Coppertone / Maybelline spokesperson. She was *the* girl. They told me about Sonny and Cher, and that Cher never ever wore dresses. At the time that was revolutionary. They told me about the Motown myths; how one of the Temptations had pulled a gun on Berry Gordy, and that Diana Ross had had his baby.

Renae was the first to graduate from high school.

Over the years they taught me so much. They were the ones who told me about Sylvester and the Cockettes. That was the first time I'd heard of Sylvester, and that he was a drag queen. For Christmas my sisters would give me books about Hollywood. They couldn't give me or tell me enough. I stored up every detail, and little did they know that they were helping to create a monster. Thanks to their example I became a magazine junkie. I used to go up to Thrifty's drugstore and spend hours just looking at magazines like *Photoplay, Rona Barrett's Hollywood,* and anything that had to do with showbiz. It was at the time Desi Arnaz, Jr. and Liza Minnelli were going out. They were the hot couple. To this day I can still pick up a magazine and be totally entertained—doubly so, if there is a picture of me inside (although to tell you the truth every queen's preference is to be on the cover rather than on the inside).

In their early teens Renae and Renetta were part of a

Even though we fought like cats and dogs, my sister Rozy was my best friend when we were growing up. She taught me how to tie my shoes.

clique of about seven or eight girls their age. They all hung out at Deborah and Aletha's house, and I used to tag along too. The thing about their place was that they had a record player. Because their mother was a maid in LaJolla she would be gone all day, so they would go over there, play all the latest records, and smoke cigarettes. Every day in the summer of sixty-seven they would have a dance party after summer school, and we would go up there and dance to "Grazin' in the Grass" by Hugh Masakela and "I Think I'm Going in Circles" by the Friends of Distinction, "Uptight" by Stevie Wonder, and "Tighten Up" by Archie Bell and the Drells. That's where I learned how to cha-cha and boogaloo. I just picked it up by hanging out with them. I've always had a sense of rhythm, so it just came natural-ly. We would also make up dance routines and teach them to other people. That's when I realized that girls were much more fun than boys. Meanwhile, my sisters were always trying to get rid of me because I was the kid brother. But, honey, there was *no* getting rid of me.

Increasingly, I was getting in touch with my feminine side shall we say. I would roll my hair in rollers and use my mother's makeup. I tried to do it in a natural way so no one could tell. Marcus Allen—who went to my school and became a famous football star—once came up to me and said, "You put a roller in your hair, didn't you?" He always knew he was going to be a football star, and I suppose I always knew I was going to be a rock and roll star. I didn't see that I had anything to hide, so I told him that yes, I had put rollers in my hair. What of it? He just muttered something about me being a sissy and walked away. The kids would always tease me about being a sissy and a queer, but they were never vicious.

When *The Partridge Family* came out, I put together a band in our neighborhood. I was the motivator. I went over to our summer clubhouse and sketched out the game plan for the new band. The other kids were never as enthusiastic about it as I was, and I could never get everyone together for rehearsals. One day I wrote a song called "Love, Love, Love," but the next week, before I could get the band together to learn it, I found out that Bobby Sherman had already released a song called "Love, Love, Love." That was a little depressing.

My sisters' pop culture lessons came to an abrupt end when they were fifteen and ran away from home, leaving me and Rozy behind with Mama. They were having trouble with my mother because they were too big for their britches: just typical teenagers who had a mother with a temper. They got caught and went to Hillcrest Receiving Home, which was a halfway house for juveniles. They lived there for a while. Then they got a foster parent, actually their high school counselor Alfreda Smith, and lived with her for about six months while they finished their high school education.

When she was sixteen, my sister Renetta started going out with my brother-in-law to be, Laurence. Laurence was a huge influence on my life, because he was the bridge between my neighborhood and the rest of the world. Laurence was ambitious, more ambitious than anyone I'd ever met before. He was the vice president of his class, and his parents were very upstanding citizens within the black community. He came up to meet my mother and said he wanted to date Renetta. Of course she cussed him out, but he didn't back off. He was carrying a briefcase, wore a suit, and seemed very together. He said that his goal was to be an executive, and he sure was pumping an executive realness look. My mother was very impressed with his stick-with-it-ness, and they became friends. Once he got in good graces with my mom he would take us all up to LaJolla, which is where all the rich people lived, in his '65 Impala low rider. His passion was looking at beautiful

Laurence and Renetta at Disneyland.

homes, and his dream was to live in one. So, on Sunday afternoons we would cruise the streets looking at the most expensive ones.

After dating for a year, Laurence and Renetta got married. She was only seventeen. My mother gave her consent, but only to spite my father who didn't want them to get married. Laurence got a scholarship to UCSD, and they lived together on campus in student housing. His plan was to become a lawyer.

Laurence also had a big record collection and was a

music aficionado. He worked at the college radio station doing some small-time promoting. Once he took me and Rozy up to L.A. to watch a taping of *Soul Train*. Later that day we went into a studio on Hollywood Boulevard where we met Little Anthony who was recording there. He had been a big star in the early sixties with his group Little Anthony and the Imperials, and was attempting a comeback. My sister and I were very excited to be in Hollywood. We had on matching outfits: very-high-waisted bellbottoms in ice cream blue, flared from the thigh down. Our pants were known as Fred Astaires because they had a big cuff on them, and with my big Afro I looked like Foster Sylver of the Sylvers. This weird promoter-producer type sidled up to me and said that I should be a singer. He had a big flashy diamond on his pinkie, and there was a sleazy air about him. That was my first taste of showbiz.

In many ways Laurence was really my ticket out of San Diego. He was a major influence on me. He educated me so much in terms of how to speak properly and how to articulate my thoughts. He would constantly correct what I was saying and grilled me like a sergeant. He was socialized in a different world than the ghetto life I grew up in.

He and Renetta became surrogate parents to me. In fact I even went to live with them. When I was kicked out of Patrick Henry High School (the school I had gone to without attending a single class), Renetta said, "You need to change your environment, why don't you come live with us out in El Cajon?" They were living in a ritzy area in a house with a swimming pool, three-car garage, the works. So I did. They had just adopted a baby, Scotty. Scotty and I were kindred spirits starting out at this new house on a new life together.

I went to Valhalla High School in El Cajon, and of the two thousand students there, I was one of five blacks. That was total culture shock for me, the first of many. I'd never lived around white people before or kids whose parents had money. That was the first time I really broke into a new clique. Those fifteen-year-olds were gnarly cats, and I

Three Sisters

taught myself how to drink beer, even though I hated it. I realized my ability to be a chameleon, to deliver what I felt people wanted from me. I became close with about three or four of those boys who would come over to Laurence's house where they could drink and do bong hits. Recently I saw the movie *Dazed and Confused*. It was a trip, because the movie was exactly what my life was like at Valhalla High—dazed and confused.

DRAG TIPS

1. Be sweet; there are enough bitchy queens.
2. Never let people see you eat.
3. Never respond to someone who refers to you as "Slim"—as in "Yo, Slim!"
4. If someone clocks you and starts to dis you, pay them no mind.
5. Matte your face at least every 30 minutes.
6. Never wear flat shoes.
7. Posture is essential. Elongate your neck. Straighten your spine.
8. Never perm your own hair.
9. Don't wear high heels in soggy grass.
10. Remember: beauty is pain.

Chapter

Hotlanta

By the summer of '76, Laurence and Renetta decided that they were moving to Atlanta, Georgia. Laurence felt he could get an advantage if he went to a black boom town on the sunbelt. San Diego was a very white and conservative Republican community, but Atlanta had a black mayor, a black senator, and was known as Chocolate City for being 64 percent black. When they asked me if I wanted to go with them, I said, "Sure, why not?" The only thing I knew about Atlanta was that Henry "Hank" Aaron, the Home Run King, was from there.

I'd been living with Laurence and Renetta for six months, and I couldn't go back to my mother's house because you can never go home again. I had spread my

*My first month in Georgia. My mother gave me the gold
necklace for good luck.*

wings and flown the nest. In the space of six short months,
although I was still a kid, I had grown up. Even when I
went back to visit, everyone seemed caught in a time warp.
My mother thought it was a good idea because Atlanta had
more to offer than my old neighborhood.

On July 23 we packed up and drove cross-country in
a '73 Mercedes. When we arrived we stayed at this
Ramada Inn overnight. The next morning Laurence called
a real estate agent to look at houses in Buckhead, an afflu-
ent area. The realtor was this white woman called Queenie
(or something royal), and because I had told her that I was
into performing she told us about the Northside School of
Performing Arts, and how it would be ideal for me.
Queenie may not have sold us a house that day, but she sold
me on getting my education. When the school year started
I was determined to go there.

But for a while we were in dire straits. Renetta was
pregnant with her baby Morgan, and we didn't have any

money. This reverend and his wife—Hattie Ruth and Reverend Joseph Stafford—ran the Free For All Baptist church. They took us in and we stayed with them until we got our feet on the ground. Eventually, Laurence got a job, and I got my wish to go to Northside School of Performing Arts.

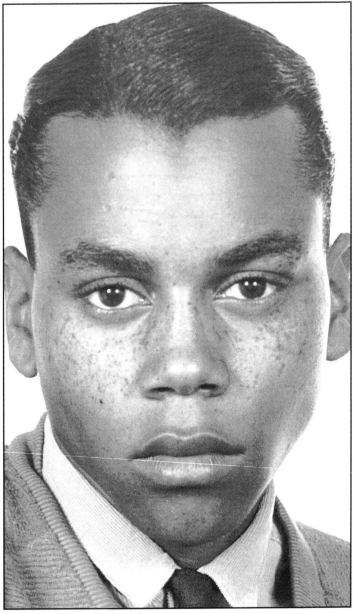

Becoming a man.

The part of me you see on stage now came alive at Northside. I was free, I was away from all the kids I grew up with. And not only that, but I was with other kids who were artistic, who had the same feelings I had. For the first time in my life I felt like I was home. Since this was the first year that they had forced integration in the schools in the South, there were also a lot of black kids there. In fact, it was strictly half black and half white. Coming from California, I had never seen so many black people. I never knew so many black people existed.

I got enrolled into the musical drama department, but it was too stiff for me. I really hit pay dirt after the first quarter when I switched over to straight drama. My teacher Bill Pannel was twenty-six years old and had just come from L.A., where he had studied with Mr. Strasberg himself. Bill was hot-headed, young, and full of cum. We were all in love with him. He was so passionate, so dynamic, and if someone was doing it wrong he'd have temper tantrums and scream, "Damn it! Get back there and do it right." He taught us Strasberg's Method acting, which is all about becoming the character from the inside out. Once you feel you are the character, fuck the lines!—at least that was my understanding of it. I remember doing these improvisations with my friend, and we'd just go off ad-libbing endlessly. We didn't know the lines, but Bill loved it. I found it so captivating because it was real, and it was raw, and I really got to explore myself.

Soon I developed a name for myself, partly because I came from California and partly because I dressed so freaky. I got on Renetta's sewing machine and made my own clothes. I would think nothing of going to school in stripes, plaid, and a cowboy hat. Everybody was like, "Whoa—what are you thinking?" I was thinking *Fame!* I was Irene Cara, and I was going to light up the sky with my name! People thought I was losing my mind. I was, and it was fantastic. So when I saw *The Rocky Horror Picture Show* as I turned sixteen, it was just in the nick of time. Because otherwise I might have lost my nerve and turned back. But, after that, there was no turning back. I just knew

I had to do something with the dreamer in me that was screaming for release. My girlfriend took me to see the movie—another example of how girls are always more in touch than boys. Since then I've seen it maybe twenty-five times. I loved the freedom of it. I also loved the weird black humor, and it was the first time I really "got" camp and that whole idea of adopting something based on how seriously it takes itself, while being totally whacked out and demented. Since then I have made its message my credo: "Don't dream it, be it!"

But there was just one tiny problem. Because I lived about eighteen miles away from the school, I would have to get a ride to the bus, take the bus, and then hitchhike when I got to the other end. In other words, I was always late for school. This might not have been such a big deal had I not flunked the tenth grade in San Diego and I had to do it over again. Finally Laurence got fed up and told me I was going to have to change schools.

"Laurence, don't do this," I said.

"Yeah, you're moving schools," he said. I begged my sister and Laurence to let me stay, but to no avail.

I was just so upset. Bill, my teacher, said, "Come here, I want to tell you something. . . . Ru, do not take life so seriously."

At that point, I was like, "What?"

He said, "Do not take life so seriously."

It took me a few years, but now I totally know what he means, and it's probably the most important thing anyone's ever told me. The point is that life is a banquet and most poor suckers are starving to death. To put your problems and anxieties into proper perspective, you need to realize that as serious as they may seem to you, compared to the plight of the rest of the world, they aren't half bad.

Andy Warhol's tip when you get upset and freaked out about something is to sit back and say, "So what?" So what? because, believe me, the rest of the Universe does not give a shit about your problems. So what? because in reality your problem is probably no big deal. And, finally, So what? because there may not be anything that you can do about it—these things often have to unravel themselves, and there is nothing you can do other than have the grace and patience to sit them out.

And I *shouldn't* have taken it all so seriously, because, as things turned out, they let me stay.

It's funny because even though Laurence and Renetta were only a few years older than me, they were my guardians and were in charge. And because they were so close to me in age, they were just coming out of this phase themselves, and so they knew the bottom line was that I was a pot-smoking, havoc-wreaking good-time boy. They were more strict with me than my mother—they had to be. But I didn't let that stop me. Laurence had a passion for cars and every six months he got a fancy schmancy new car—somehow. This was fine by me because in high school I would take my friends, many of whom came from rich families, to concerts in Rolls-Royces. Rarely did I get permission. I would wait for Laurence and Renetta to go to bed, then I would sneak out of the house and roll their Porsche—or whatever it was that week—down the hill so they couldn't hear it. Then I would start up the engine, drive into Buckhead, and park

PHOTO SHOOT TIPS

1. Have a good night's sleep before the shoot. (Although I never do! I always get insomnia!)
2. Insist on having a mirror right next to the camera so you can play off it.
3. Make sure the lighting is as close to the camera as possible.
4. Have the flash and the camera coming from the same direction.
5. Never allow a photographer to shoot you from below unless it's a full-body shot from across the room.
6. Try to imagine a person or a place that will give you the desired expression.
7. Study *Vogue* and *Harper's Bazaar* in advance so you can have some posing ideas.
8. Relax your forehead.
9. Make sure the photographer has either a computer to do retouching or a budget for airbrushing.
10. Keep your eyes open and have Visine on hand for redness.
11. Bring the music you like to set the mood.
12. Make sure you see the Polaroid tests.
13. Bring an assistant!
14. Don't rely on stylists for clothing. Bring your own stuff as well.
15. Put lots of gauze over the lens!

outside the local bar called The Place on Paces, where I would get stoned with my high school friends, sitting out front. Because in the South people are a lot more loose and hot to trot, there were lots of wild experiences. Later that night—sometimes as the sun was coming up—I would drive home and get a quick couple of hours sleep before heading back to school, with no one any the wiser.

It was around this time that I started to get my education in other things—let's call it career orientation. In San Diego I'd seen some drag queens and transsexuals hanging around, but I never really thought anything of it. The first time I got to know anyone like that was on the bus to school when I was in the tenth grade. Every morning there was this transvestite waiting at the bus stop. I remember thinking wow, how weird! She used to work nights at a sex club up the street called The Down Under. So when I was on my way to school in the morning, she was on her way home. She always wore purple, and we used to talk about this and that, like the weather.

Soon after making her acquaintance, I also saw my first drag queen performing. It was Crystal Labajia at Numbers Disco. The year was 1978. She was on the dance floor doing a Donna Summer song, and she had on a black bustier bikini thing with black fishnets and big black hair. The illusion was so incredible I was fooled, and thought to myself, "Is that Donna Summer? Is she really singing?" Of course she was lipsynching, but I couldn't believe it, I just couldn't believe it. After that I saw all the queens performing: Ashley Nicole, Charlie Brown, Lily White, Tina Devore, Dina Jacobs, and Yetiva Antoinette, who was the fiercest of them all. All the black queens were very current. They did looks that were up to the minute and performed the latest songs, while for the most part the white queens were more traditional. They did sappy things like show tunes from *A Chorus Line*.

As my draguacation took off, my academic career nose-dived. Having scraped through tenth grade at Northside, I went to a school in South Fulton County for the eleventh grade, where I finally dropped out. Kids, do not do this! Stay in school! Meanwhile my brother-in-law's ambitions to become a lawyer also seemed to have gone off the rails, and he had gotten into the car business instead. Just shy of seventeen, I threw myself wholeheartedly into his company as his man Friday. He was a car broker and would sell Mercedes, Rolls-Royces, Jaguars, Porsches—any expensive car, because they had high profit margins. He would send me to the library to go through the newspaper classifieds from all over the country, looking for cars and circling the ones I thought were good. Then he'd call, make a deal, and I'd fly out to Kansas City—or wherever—with a check draft to pick up the car, which I would then drive back for him to resell. I was never good at selling the cars. Too honest, I guess.

I worked for Laurence off and on for about five years and traveled all over the United States. I probably drove by myself from Atlanta to San Diego well over a hundred times in a car. It was really good for me to see the country, and I sang the whole time—training my voice.

Chapter 7

If It Ain't Fun, Don't Do It

It was the summer of '81. I was wondering how my life was going to unfold, and how I was going to become a star. The answer came when I stumbled upon this weird cable program called *The American Music Show*. It was basically a variety show consisting of skits with a sick sense of humor performed by a kooky cast. As I wrote the credits down on the back of an envelope, I discovered that it was produced by a company called Funtone.

The Funtone group came out of the early seventies. They were a bunch of writers and artists who all met up when they were working on the McGovern presidential campaign in '72. Subsequently they started a comedy troupe called Red Meat and Sprouts, very much like an

On the road to stardom.

alternative *Saturday Night Live*. They also launched a record label called Funtone Records. The corporation has two mottoes: "Fight Boredom" and "If It Ain't Fun, Don't Do It." I have tried to live my life according to both those golden rules. Soon after they started doing their improv skits, public access started. Public access meant that by law the cable operators had to provide one or two channels to the community for people to make their own programs. These programs could be made by anyone about anything.

I am sure that the bright spark in Washington who thought up this concept imagined an endless series of worthy but dull shows about local rotary meetings. The last thing he would have imagined would have been a bunch of old hippies and drag queens seizing the airwaves. If he had I am sure the idea of public access would have remained an idea. But it didn't, and not only are we the richer for it, but for me it was my launch pad.

The American Music Show was taped in Dick Richard's place, which was this really hippified house with funky kitsch things all over the place. It became Funtone HQ. The show was hosted by Dick Richards, James Bond, Pam Perry, Bud and Holly, and Potsy Duncan. It featured all these incredible guests with unbelievable multiple personas. Paul Burke played Ralph Bailey, Duffy Odum, and a whole bunch of other characters. He once tried to illustrate the concept of cable television with an anatomical map of the human spine. Molly Worthington looked like a Cher from India, and she created the sick character, LaWanda Peak. Later I discovered LaWanda Peak had two sisters, Starla Peak and Deaundra Peak (who in real life was the fabulous Rosser). They lived in a trailer park and had, as they put it, the "gift of voice." Well they were like the Andrews Sisters on acid. Bad acid. When they sang— as they insisted on doing—they would all scream, holler, and screech at once, out of time and out of tune. Genius, pure genius. Then there was Jon Witherspoon, who was known in drag as Lahoma Van Zandt, David Goldman whose alter ego is the cocktail-slugging Betty Jack Divine, and the band the Now Explosion, who consisted of Elouise Montague Cougar Mellancamp, Lady Clare, Lizette Quatro Christian, and Larry Tee. The list just goes on and on. I guess there were about twenty of them altogether.

When I saw those guys on public access I thought, "That's where I belong." I knew these were the people who would get my sense of humor and understand what I was doing. I vowed to get to these people by any means necessary, and sent in a picture of myself and a letter saying that I'd like to be on the show. One day while I was home Paul

Burke called me and invited me on the show. I couldn't believe he was calling me, because in my mind he was a star. Meanwhile they couldn't believe I had written them a letter. When they read it they were falling about screaming, "Oh, my God, somebody wants to be on our show!"

I will always regard writing that letter to Dick as my start in showbiz, and as one of the most important things that I ever did in my life. However, the sixty-four-million-dollar question was, What was I going to do once I got on the show? Fate took care of that. I had just left the downtown library when I found twenty dollars on the street. I thought, "Great! I'm gonna go have myself a drink." I went to a bar and the waitress who waited on me was a living doll. Her name was Robin, and we became friends. She had a two-year-old little boy and a roommate named Josette. She needed some help to move into her new apartment, so I helped her out by driving the U-Haul truck. As we were driving I said to her, "We should start a group called RuPaul and the U-Hauls, and you guys can come on *The American Music Show* with me."

I made costumes for us on my sister's sewing machine and we did a dance routine that we had rehearsed all week to "Shot Gun" by Junior Walker and the All Stars. It went off without a hitch. After the show they interviewed us. Dick really liked us, and we became a fixture on the show immediately.

So, in January of '82, with that appearance on *The American Music Show,* I officially started my show business career. Of course not everyone would regard an outing on public access as the "business," but from *Wayne's World* to *Coffee Talk,* so many of the skits on *Saturday Night Live* are parodies of public access shows—and often the original is better. For me it was the equivalent of Roseanne's first appearance on Johnny Carson, or the Beatles' debut on Ed Sullivan. Okay, the audience share was not of the same magnitude, but you couldn't tell me that. Show business for me is a state of mind. If you want to be a star, you just need to believe that you are one. When I appeared on Dick's show my star was born, and it really made no dif-

ference whether millions were watching or just a handful of cable subscribers.

Something else was important about it too. Up to that point in my life I was all dressed up with no place to go. I felt the creative juices flowing within me, but had no idea in which direction to channel them. *The American Music Show* showed me the way. I was a child of television. As someone who had grown up watching as much of it as possible, whenever possible, I belonged on television. I was never at a loss for things to say, and from my years of study I instinctively knew just how to turn the volume up, how to pitch myself, and how to speak in sound bites. In short, I knew how to speak the language of television. Fluently.

That spring I was invited to a party at the Inman Park Festival that everyone was going to. I showed up with my bleached blond hair driving this huge four-door Mercedes Benz. Jon Witherspoon was making a movie about prostitutes starring Lady Clare from the Now Explosion. I said to them, "I have this big car. Maybe I can drive by, be a john, and pick her up." But they were like, "Oh, uh, right."

You know how everyone is when a new person comes into a clique, it's like, "Who does she think she is?" I've never been good with cliques. Cliques are all about people trying to find security in groups. "Oh, I'm special now because I'm part of this clique." But it's really just the emperor's new clothes. People aren't really together in cliques, and the sense of security that they feel is just an illusion. Eventually, all cliques disintegrate. That's why I've always felt secure in my insecurity.

Before I left the party that night I distinctly remember making some sort of speech: "Guys, remember my name 'cause I am a star, and this isn't the last you'll see of me blah blah blah . . ." and I drove off into the night in my lime green Mercedes.

Of course, it wasn't the last they saw of me because Dick asked us back on *The American Music Show* again and again and again. Sometimes we would take the instrumental version of a song like "Too Busy to Think About My Baby" by Orbit and rap my live vocals on top of it.

The Now Explosion wedding: My first time in glamour drag. Bottom row from left to right: Eloise Montague, Potsy Duncan, Reina, Ann Cox. Top row left to right: Russ Trent, Tom Zarelli, Judy LaGrange, Larry Tee, Steven Stubbs, Jon Witherspoon, Lady Clare, Paul Burke, Molly Worthington, David Klemchek, Robert Warren, Todd Butler, me (notice my feet hanging off the shoes).

Other times I would come on as a guest, talking or showing videos that I made myself. At one point they did a spin-off show called *Dancerama USA*. I got a big break on that show with a segment called "Learn a Dance with RuPaul." It was a new wave *American Bandstand*.

Gradually, as the Now Explosion warmed up to me, I would do things with them. It was during one of these special appearances that I stumbled unwittingly on my future—although it would take almost another ten years for

My third appearance on The American Music Show. *From left to right: Dick Richards, me, James Bond.*

me to claim it. As a gimmick the Now Explosion had a wedding in one of their shows, and Lahoma and Lady Clare got married on stage. All their friends who were guys dressed up as bridesmaids, and all their friends who were girls dressed up as guys. Not to state the obvious, I dressed up as a girl. Believe it or not it was the first time I did real drag in a dress, heels, and with hair; I had never worn tits before, I'd never shaved my legs before, or even worn a wig before.

Honey, the impact it had on people was amazing. But the impact it had on me was even more amazing. I honestly didn't know I had a great pair of legs until I got into drag and slipped on those pumps. Even after this first drag experience, it took years of experimentation before I landed in the glamour drag that started paying my bills. If in my mind's eye I always knew I was going to be a star, I never thought it was going to be as a drag queen. The thought never crossed my mind.

Around the same time I started putting up posters all over Atlanta. It really made me famous there 'cause

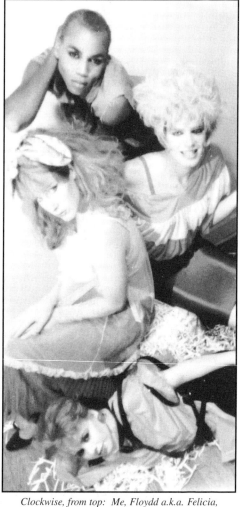

Clockwise, from top: Me, Floydd a.k.a. Felicia, Lori Nevada, and Bunny Hickory Dickory Dock.

Ru goes Bow Wow Wow.

no one else (apart from the Now Explosion) was doing posters. I took pictures of myself and blew them up by Xeroxing them. I didn't have a budget for airbrushing, so I would do it myself by taking a pencil eraser to shape up the outlines, white out those unsightly marks, and, using my own natural artistry, enhance the eyes. Then I would slap on a slogan like "RuPaul Is Red Hot" or "RuPaul Is Everything," make 200 copies, and plaster Midtown armed with a paint brush and a bucket of wheat paste.

Generally the slogans were borrowed from other places. One of my favorites was from *the* Donna Summer album *Donna Summer*. It read: "This is the hottest summer on record." Isn't that genius? For Donna Summer, the hottest summer on record. Another of my favorites, "The future belongs to those who can hear it coming," was on David Bowie's *Heroes* LP. I took that and made it, "The future belongs to those who can *smell* it coming." I've always loved clever advertising slogans, like the ones Samantha came up with on the TV show *Bewitched*.

Funny enough, some of the people I have shared this detail of my career with have been quite shocked and said, "What, you didn't make them up yourself?" Of course not! The point about pop culture is that so much of it is borrowed. There's very little that's brand new. Instead, creativity today is a kind of shopping process—picking up on and sampling things from the world around you, things you grew up with. That's very much my modus operandi. If you knew all the references, you could deconstruct one of my performances and place every look, every word, and every move. I do. I know all the references, and watching myself on tape I love to sit with friends and unstitch (to their amazement) the patchwork of my performance, identifying this bit from here and this bit from there. I really see myself as a sampling machine. Even the supermodel drag queen I would later become is a kind of Frankenstein's monster—a collage made up of bits and pieces from old television shows, copies of *Vogue* magazine, and advertisements. I think at this late stage in the twentieth century it's almost all been done, and everything now is a kind of rehash. My life and my work is really just a question of filling in the blanks and coloring by numbers.

The posters were a huge success and helped establish me in Atlanta. By that summer I had gotten enough money together to get my own apartment in Midtown with my friend Cathy, who later changed her name to Carson, who later changed her name to Cabbage—it was a punk thing. Shortly after Cabbage and I moved in together, I met up with other kids who had moved to Midtown Atlanta from the sticks of suburbia in search of something. Like John Ingle, who would later become renowned as the "Lady" Bunny. She was straight off the bus from Chattanooga, and without doubt the sharpest wit I ever met. He had me in stitches. Like Floydd, who was Bryan Chambers then, but

RuPAUL'S FAVORITE DRAG QUEEN MOVIES

1. *Mahogany:* I live for the modeling montage.
2. *Paris Is Burning:* The film that inspired *Supermodel (You Better Work).*
3. *Valley of the Dolls:* The rise and fall of three queens and their hair.
4. *Funny Face:* Kay Thompson is brilliant—think pink!
5. *Rocky Horror Picture Show:* Don't dream it, be it.
6. *Torch Song:* Joan Crawford in blackface with red hair!
7. *Priscilla, Queen of the Desert:* Fun-loving road picture.
8. *What a Way to Go:* Shirley MacLaine has a million Edith Head costumes.
9. *Cleopatra Jones:* At 12 I wanted to be Tamara Dobson.
10. *Mommie Dearest:* Ups and downs of being a queen.
11. *All About Eve:* Bette Davis—Strong as a man, made like a woman.
12. *A Streetcar Named Desire:* Misunderstood queen caught in reality.
13. *Vertigo:* Girlfriend gets clocked.
14. *Auntie Mame:* Life is a banquet and most drag queens are stuffing their faces.
15. *Stage Door:* Queens trying to make it on the Great White Way.

fresh out of high school and looking for trouble. Although Floydd is one of my dearest friends today, we didn't really like each other at first because we were both know-it-alls. The question would come up, "What movie was it when Bette Davis says 'What a dump'?" And we'd both simultaneously say *"Beyond the Forest"* and look at each other thinking, "I can't stand this guy."

I would wear makeup and spike my hair in various new wave styles. The first wig I ever got was from Lady Clare in the Now Explosion. She had tons of wigs. After she gave me one she couldn't stop—she gave me another, and another, and another. I would pile them up and wear all of them at once in an Elvira-type thing. It wasn't officially drag yet. It was punk or gender fuck drag. I wasn't being fashionable, I was being hooty; bad wigs and thrift store clothes *and* size-ten Candies, with my feet hanging all out the back. In my mind I was hot, so I was hot, and you know what? Men would love it! Men don't care, they really don't, as long as you have the stuff on they don't care. They're really into the paraphernalia, the accoutrements.

And I was fearless. The South has always been a hotbed of racial tension and a stronghold for the Ku Klux Klan. From time to time they march, heavily protected by the National Guard, and from time to time everybody else marches against them, also heavily protected by the National Guard. Decked out in all my grunge drag—jockstrap, fishnets, high heels, and a humongous Mohawk—I went on a march in Forsythe County. When I told people I was going, everybody thought I was mad. If anyone was going to get lynched by the Klan everybody thought I was the number-one candidate. But, you know, while marching up the street, I looked over the shoulder of the National Guardsmen and into the eyes of one of the Klansmen. And our eyes locked. I realized then that many of them probably liked Michael Jackson's *Thriller* album, Häagen-Dazs ice cream, and springtime in Georgia. What's the brouhaha? I understood then that my uniqueness was not just a spectacle for its own sake. When I looked that person in the eyes I realized that I was looking at myself. He had found a way to bring attention to himself and validate himself. And so had I. No matter what uniform we may be wearing, underneath it all we are all the same—unique individuals, alone, aching to belong. Ultimately, we all have more in common with each other than we don't have in common. That's all.

I started doing shows at this punk club TV Dinner, where Dick and the *American Music Show* crew were hanging out. It was there that I had my first hit of acid. It was incredible. I did a lot of LSD from ages twenty to thirty. Once a week. At least. It was such an easy drug to do: cheap, fun, therapeutic. I was able to see myself in this detached way and turn the volume up on my subconscious, although in the end unconscious is all I became.

I started popping pills when I was fourteen. Reds were the big things. They're barbiturates, downers, and they make you feel like you're on heroin. I remember as a kid seeing a girl OD on reds in the park. Still, I never thought twice about taking pills. I thought that was the way it was supposed to be. "Feeling down? Take a pill!" Of course anyone could be forgiven for thinking that, just watch TV; if you have indigestion, a headache, feeling fat or simply tired—take a pill! Taking drugs is a symptom of something else. Simply eliminating the drugs does not eliminate the something else, and usually that something else is you. You feel insecure, you feel like crap, and you want out. Drugs are a handy escape. If the government really wanted to stop drugs, they should not take away a person's sense of self-esteem, sense of worth, and dignity. And one more thing. When the drug issue comes up in the media, there's something that everybody knows but never owns up to: Drugs can be *fun*.

When it comes to drugs, you name it, I've done it. Heroin's a yucky drug—just like having some sleeping powder. It's like bad Ecstasy. I never shot up. Mercifully, sticking needles in my arm never appealed to me. Cocaine is the worst drug I've ever taken, and I particularly didn't like the evil person that came out when I was freebasing. Special K has to be a close second because it's nauseous stuff; it makes you so disoriented you can't even walk. You have to hold onto the wall. Everything's weaving. You

turn a flip inside your own body, and you don't know where you are or what's going on.

You want to know the truth about drugs? You can only go one or two ways. You can go up, or you can go down. That's it. After a certain point, though, no matter what you do, what you take, you don't go anywhere, and that's when you've got to sit down and face yourself.

Chapter 8

Wee Wee Pole

After a year of working the Midtown club scene with the U-Hauls, out of the blue these two high school kids, Robert Warren and Todd Butler, came to me with the idea of starting a band. So we started playing music together. We called the band Wee Wee Pole. We chose "wee wee" because it was cute, and "pole" just sort of happened. It also sort of sounds like Ru Ru Paul. We all wrote the music, and I usually wrote the lyrics.

We'd rehearse after school at Todd's parents' house. Their door was always open, and I would go over and raid their well-stocked refrigerator, which was a junk-food addict's dream.

After rehearsing for about a month we got our first

gig, opening for the Now Explosion. Eventually, we became pretty popular ourselves. Throughout eighty-three we performed all over the East Coast, taking the gigs wherever we could get them. The lineup consisted of Robert on bass guitar, Todd on guitar, David Klemchek on percussion, and me on vocals. Sometimes

RuPaul and the U-Hauls reunion.
Left to right: Gina, me, and Chrissie.

we would have the U-Hauls up there with us. At this point the U-Hauls had changed over to these two other girls, Chrissie and Gina. They were about 250 pounds each and five-four, and were the quintessential U-Hauls, the famous ones!

The sound was new wave tribal melodies. At the time my look was very Bow Wow Wow. I was wearing a Mohawk and did jungle looks, like Tarzan. I wore a loin-cloth and war paint. The show was designed to entertain, Vegas-style. There were costume changes, choreographed dances, and a gimmick I stole from Prince's group, the Time. A valet would come on stage between numbers with a mirror so I could fix my makeup and then run off. During the numbers themselves I would hoot and holler all over the

stage and do all these wild things, like run out into the
audience with this big stuffed pole. About twelve inches in
diameter, this big round thing was our wee wee pole, our
mascot. It was brown and it had flowers on it (it was actually part of a couch). Once I went out into the audience
waving this thing around and knocked a table over. Later I
learned that someone's foot had been broken when the
table fell. I remember playing with Wee Wee Pole at a club

Me and Floydd, Christmas '84.

in Birmingham, Alabama called the Cavern. The only black person in the club was me! I remember making comments about it, but the audience loved it. On another occasion a couple met at our show and later got married—such was the power of the wee wee pole.

In September that year Wee Wee Pole traveled to New York and performed at Danceteria, thanks to Ruth Polsky, who booked talent at the club. I met her at a party the Now Explosion had given for New Order. They were on tour, Ruth was their tour manager, and they all took a liking to me. At their urging Ruth said, "If you ever want to play New York, give me a call." So I did, and she gave us a gig. I became her pet project, and she was very good to me.

After we played New York, we went in the studio and recorded some songs—"Tarzan," "In My Neighborhood," and "Body Heat." But then in December we broke up. It was perfectly amicable. Robert's thinking was you should only be in a band for a year, and if it doesn't happen in that time, you should move on. Because he had been in bands before, and because he was a really good bass player, I respected what he had to say. So, he went to join another band, and eventually the songs we recorded ended up on my first album, *Sex Freak*.

I found myself without my band, and I said to myself what does a star do when the band breaks up? You write a book and you start making movies of course!

It so happened that Laurence had just bought a video camera, which was just what I needed to start my film career. I asked Jon Witherspoon to film me in a movie called *Trilogy of Terror*. It was a parody of a 1975 Karen Black TV movie, and we filmed it at his house. In the film a little blue boy statuette becomes possessed and chases me around the apartment. Jon has a collection of blue boys, so as the piece went on they started changing, getting bigger and more sinister. It was the beginning of my film career and the first of the *Trilogy of Terror* series. In the sequel *Terror 2*, I was joined by my costars Lady Bunny and Floydd. It was basically the same story as the first, but this time it was three girls in a house being chased around by an

FAVORITE MUSIC
VIDEOS—DRAG

1. *Ashes to Ashes,* David Bowie
2. *I'll Be Your Shelter,* Taylor Dayne
3. *Show Some Respect,* Tina Turner
4. *If I Could Turn Back Time,* Cher
5. *Chain Reaction,* Diana Ross
6. *So Emotional,* Whitney Houston
7. *Running Back to You,* Vanessa Williams
8. *My Lovin' (You're Never Gonna Get It),* En Vogue
9. *Love on Top of Love,* Grace Jones
10. *Sweet and Low,* Deborah Harry

unseen sinister evil. We did it as a trailer with Dick Richards doing the voice-over. *Terror 3D* reunited the same team in an hour-long thriller with the three of us in a bigger house terrorized by a hatchet-faced demon and murdered one by one. Since I was the star, I was murdered last.

These films brought me a certain amount of notoriety and kept my name up in lights, but they weren't putting food on the table. So I wrote a book. You may say pamphlet, I say it's a book. I had already been making postcards of myself, which I would sell for fifty cents in clubs, and decided to take it one step further. The book was called *If You Love Me Give It to Me.* First I put twenty blank pieces of paper on the floor, then I put a full-page picture of myself on every other page. Then I put a picture on the cover, and a picture on the back cover, and filled in the remaining blank pages with dialogue and anecdotes. I basically went over my life story, what I believed in, my favorite things, my favorite food—everything. I sold them in clubs for two dollars apiece, and went through the first printing in an evening. It was such a hit that I went on to publish four more different titles: *If You Love Me, Give It to Me One More Time, RuPaul—Your Guide to Health, Beauty and Nigger Love, New York Is a Big Fat Greasy Ho,* and *Freak Sex.*

My books kept me fluid but not enough to prevent me from being evicted from my apartment come January of 1984. So there I was, a successful author, pop star and TV star, homeless and penniless. By that fall I had become fast friends with the new kid on the scene, Jon Ingle. He later became Bunny Hickory Dickory Dock and then, in New York, the "Lady" Bunny. We were inseparable and we were even homeless together. During those three to four months we would roam the streets of Midtown together all night, getting into trouble with black guys, taking them behind buildings and getting them to show us their dicks. It was just horny partying around. We would say, "Can we feel it?" They'd say, "Yes," and we would just laugh and take off running. During the day we

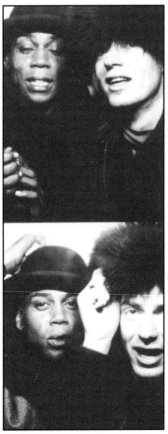

Buddy picture: Bryan Felicia Frank Floydd Chambers and me.

would crash in all these different places: friends' houses, abandoned cars, Piedmont Park, wherever. Being homeless is much easier when you're young. Eventually, Floydd, Bunny, and me got an apartment together at Tenth and Juniper. It became the party house.

Midtown Atlanta was probably the closest thing to Haight Ashbury I've ever seen. In the sixties and seventies it was the hub of bohemian lifestyles—hippies, rock 'n roll, the whole shebang. The area dates back to the Civil War, when it was called the Tight Squeeze because there was a drainage problem. It was a place where the misfits of the war, the lost and the wounded, would wind up. It was Misfitsville, and I fit right in. The gay community was also there, and all the artists too, because of the affordable housing. There was a go-go club called Cheetah 3, and guys would come into town, go to the club, get horny, and then look for the hookers hanging out in the vicinity. In addition to Cheetah 3, TV Dinner, Weekends, Illusions, Backstreet were all within a four-block radius. Across the way the male hustlers were up and down Cypress Street. You could get pot, you could get drugs, you could get whatever you wanted. You could even get the cops! They were not like cops in other places. They were very friendly, and you could walk down the street in drag, no problem. I tell you, it was happening.

Chapter 9

New York Is a Big, Fat, Greasy Ho

New York still beckoned, and so that summer I put together a revue called "RuPaul is Red Hot." I got Floydd—who was called Felicia at this point—Bunny, Opal Fox, and the Lady Pecan as costars. We went up to New York and did our show at the Pyramid.

The Pyramid was a neighborhood bar in the East Village where everybody went—gay, straight, artist, famous models, actors, and, on weekends, transy cruisers galore. It was a totally mixed, really fun bar that was wild every night of the week. To us southern queens it was like a home away from home. For a start the place was run by kindred southern spirits like Sister Dimension. All the queens were there—Tabboo, Hapi Phace, and Ethyl

Jungle fever.

Eichelberger—and they were doing that same gender fuck thing that we were doing. It was drag Mecca, and they even had drag queens dancing on the bar. In short, it felt like a slice of Georgia in New York City.

The new drag, or superdrag as I liked to call it, came out of punk and parodied all that was held dear in our society. Of course, the ultimate sacred cow in respectable cul-

DRAG PURSE CONTENTS

1. Compact
2. Lipstick
3. Condoms
4. Car and house keys
5. Super glue
6. Sunglasses
7. Hair pick
8. Cash/cab fare
9. Heat-seeking missile
10. Tic Tacs
11. Mace

ture is this idea of a woman as, on the one hand, glamourous and fierce as portrayed by the TV and movie stars, and, on the other hand, as housewife and slave to the kitchen. The combination of the two is a whole treasure chest of imagery ripe for parodying and celebrating, and that was what the drag queens at the Pyramid were all about.

When the run was over, Bunny and Lady Pecan both decided to stay in New York, as did Floydd and I, even though we had no place to live. Since the Pyramid was our hub, we kept our luggage there in the lockers downstairs. Hardly any time seemed to have passed since the last time I was homeless.

I worked at the Pyramid as a go-go dancer for forty dollars a night. I really honed my go-go skills there. It wasn't about the dancing, because you danced on the bar and that was only two feet wide, so there certainly wasn't very much room to maneuver. No, it was all about the attitude. Now at that time in New York people didn't tip go-go dancers like they did back home in Georgia. I decided to change that. I didn't just dance, I worked my whole body and did seductive things. When I caught someone's eye I would lick my finger and point at them and say, "Come here, I have something to say to you, big boy!" And when they came over I'd say, "Give me a dollar," and they'd say, "What for?" And I'd say, "It's good luck," and so they'd say, "Okay" and that was that. It worked like a charm, and that's exactly what it was, my southern charm shining through the smoky disco. I worked the crowd, really worked it. At weekends I would go home with sixty dollars just in tips alone. Most of the other queens didn't work it like I did. They just got up on the bar with a "la-di-dah-let's-just-get-this-over-with-and-give-me-my-forty-dollars-thank-you-very-much."

The Pyramid in its heyday was a sight to behold. A

bunch of twisted queens pumping this sick look all crammed up on this tiny bar working a room that was no bigger than your average living room—and no taller than one either. Most of us bigger gals had to duck the entire time or get a sprinkler stuck in our wig. A lot of us thought we could work on that bar forever. Little did we

know that after we had been there for a month or two our shininess wore off, management got bored, new queens emerged, and the cycle continued. Still, we could keep our stuff stored in the basement of the Pyramid even if we weren't working. We would go there seven nights a week and it was always fun.

Floydd and I became partners in crime, and looked out for one another. Most times we met someone and managed to hustle a place to stay. We had different methods. Floydd would get people to let us stay at their house 'cause they wanted to have sex with him. My commodity was never my sexuality, it was always my name. People knew I was RuPaul, and I think they let us stay at their house because they thought that maybe, just maybe, I was gonna be a star.

We also met Nelson, a childhood friend of Dick Richards who went everywhere with a video camera. Nelson had come from a grand old family in the deep South to write his novel. But once he got to Manhattan he was so taken by the exploding downtown scene that he rushed out and bought a video camera instead. He taped everyone and everything, and we all called him the Video Vampire. That camera was like a pirate's parrot. Nelson was our New York liaison, and he introduced us to the city. Every time I walk around New York I think about him all the time. He taught us about the West Village, about Fire Island, and he introduced us to Tennessee Williams movies. He was our gay educator and taught us about our birthright, our cultural inheritance. And he always supported me, no matter what. So Nelson would always let us stay at his house, but, because we knew we could, we wanted to use it sparingly.

Often Floydd and I stayed across from the Pyramid in Tompkins Square Park. We also stayed in Central Park. It was perfectly safe because we would be up all night and sleep during the day. At that time Floydd and I really became close friends and soul brothers. Come December we thought we might as well go back down South for Christmas. Bunny stayed behind and took New York by storm. She became queen of the Pyramid, and then queen of Manhattan.

When I got back to Atlanta, Dick offered me a record contract with Funtone records, and so I started recording *Sex Freak*. In retrospect, I wish I hadn't called it that. The title was meant to say that I am a sexual oddity, an androgyne. People saw it as something else, like, "I'm a sex freak, a freak for sex." Well if you have read this far, that's one thing you will know that I am not. That's all. I am not going to get drawn into steamy revelations.

In May I got an offer from the Theatrical Outfit, a local theater, to do *The Rocky Horror Picture Show*. That summer for four months I played Riff Raff the butler. It was a smash success. We ended up doing forty-five or so performances, with two shows on Friday and Saturday night and a matinee on Sunday. Although everyone in Atlanta had heard of me, this gave me more credibility, more cachet—but not more cash. Frankly, at this point I must say that my path to money, success, fame, and glamour had been a long and winding one. Although all the detours along the way built character, between you and me a more direct route to the top would have been welcome.

During that time the club next door, Weekends, asked if I would be a go-go dancer there. I did that four nights a week for two and a half years. I started at fifty dollars a night, then I went up to sixty, and then the last year I made seventy-five dollars a night, which was good for Atlanta. Mind you there was a price to pay. Every night some drunk would hit on me and grab my crotch. I couldn't stand it, but I just had to deal with it. It got to the point where I couldn't get up on that box without a drink. I couldn't beat 'em, so I joined them.

During this period I became friends with Larry Tee of the Now Explosion for the first time. I had always been wary of him. But when Now Explosion broke up, he became a deejay at Weekends when I was go-go dancing there. Because we'd get off work at the same time, we'd go and have breakfast together. He was really at a vulnerable point, and for the first time I really warmed up to him. Once he was telling me about a story he read in *People* magazine where this boy wanted to surprise his family for Christmas by climbing down the chimney like Santa Claus. Well, he got stuck and he ended up suffocating. There was this poor kid trying to do something good for his family, and it ended in tragedy. As he was telling me that story, he started crying. When someone shows himself like that, how can you resist opening up to them? And I was like, "There you are, I finally see the real you." We became really good friends after that.

With the money I was earning from go-go dancing I got a new apartment in Midtown. I moved in right next door to these two guys named Fred and Grant. Grant was

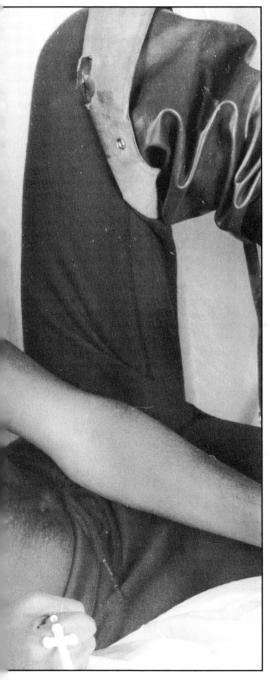

nicknamed Spicy, but Fred didn't have a nickname, and since he didn't look like a Fred to me, I renamed him Trade. I put them in my act as the new U-Hauls, although I didn't call them the U-Hauls any-more, just Spicy and Trade.

Hot child in the city.

Chapter 10

Starrbooty

In January of eighty-six Starrbooty was born. The idea came from nowhere. I was busy promoting *Sex Freak* at the time and went on Spencer Thornton's television show in the spring. I had known him for years, and he started out the interview by saying: "RuPaul, I've called you outrageous before, I've called you fabulous, what should I call you now?"

And I said, "Baby, just call me Starrbooty."

We must have laughed for a good solid five minutes, just wondering where that came from. I had never said that before, but as soon as I had I thought, "Damn that's good! I'm going to use that."

So I got together with Jon Witherspoon and asked him

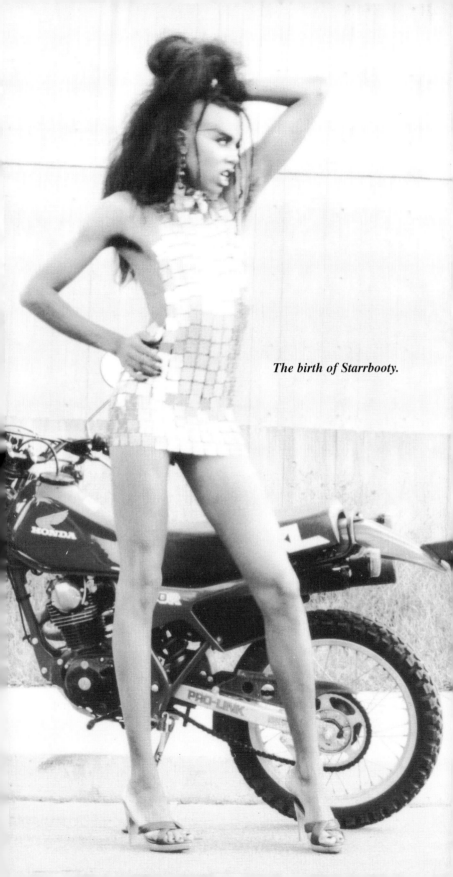

The birth of Starrbooty.

to film a new movie. It wanted to do a takeoff on the blacksploitation movies of the seventies, and I was going to call it *Starrbooty*. We did three of them in the end. In *Starrbooty I,* I played a crime fighter whose mission was to put away these crack addicts who have kidnapped the President's son. In *Starrbooty II,* my sister Cornisha Ripperton had been killed by a pimp, and so I had to go undercover as a prostitute, infiltrate his organization, and bring him down hard. In *Starrbooty III,* the singing Peak sisters kidnapped Trade and held him hostage in return for a multi-million-dollar record contract. Starrbooty rescues Trade and shows the Peaks the way to stardom by producing their first album.

Larry Tee and I wrote a bunch of songs for *Starrbooty the Motion Picture Soundtrack,* and I recorded it in New York with the Pop Tarts producing. The Pop Tarts were rather like the Pet Shop Boys only sicker, much sicker. The whole thing from start to finish was done in three days over Memorial Day weekend. Robert Warren came in and we laid down a track that was me riffing on some of my favorite slogans like, "Peanut butter head suck my dick, your mama's in the kitchen cooking thirty-minute shit, your daddy's in jail raising hell, and your sister's on the corner selling pussy for sale." For my money the real hook of the album was *The Theme Song From Starrbooty,* in which I did a kind of macho trailer-style voiceover: "Coming soon, to a theater near you! Starrbooty! Badder than Bond, more bullets than Rambo!" Talk about Method acting. But the kicker of the song was this insane chorus that just went:

Starrbooty, Starrbooty, Starrbooty, yeah
Starrbooty, Starrbooty, Starrbooty, nooo

Over and over. It was—it is—insane! It's simple and stupid, and that's how the best pop records are made by keeping them simple and stupid.

Later that summer I went back to Manhattan to promote the record at the New Music Seminar. The seminar

Beyond Thunderdome.

was being held in the Marriott Marquis, this massive twenty-first-century hotel, very corporate and glitzy, with a giant atrium. I just grabbed a bunch of records and stood in the middle and started making a scene. And when I turn it on, it's like bees to honey. I am a magnet. By this time I had turned the volume right up on my tribal look. I was doing football shoulder pads, wild voodoo-style makeup, with

"Fuck Off" and "Asshole" written on my arms as tattoos. And apart from that I was butt naked, except for a tiny jock strap and thigh-high wader boots. It was my not-yet-ready-for-MTV look. Security tried to escort me off the premises, but neither I nor the crowd was having any of it.

That was during the day. By night I worked the clubs and played at the Saint with Spicy and Trade backing me up. Back

Bustin' out of Atlanta.

then there wasn't much of a difference between what I wore in the day and what I wore in the night. Everything on my back I made myself. I shredded dozens of white plastic Hefty bags into ribbons and attached them to my shoulder pads. The end

result was a massive mop come to life. Although I called it gender fuck drag, my friend Nelson was of the opinion that it was terror drag. I suppose if you hadn't seen *The Rocky Horror Picture Show* it was pretty frightening.

We also played at Danceteria, and that was

Apocalypse drag.

the last time I saw Ruth Polsky, because a few weeks later a cab went out of control just outside Limelight nightclub, and plowed into the crowd waiting to get inside. Ruth was pinned underneath the cab and died. I was stunned by the news of her death. Not only did I lose a dear friend, I lost my closest ally in New York City. She really did help me out, and thanks to her efforts the album became a cult hit and charted in Rockpool, the grunge college chart. That was the first time I'd ever had anything on the chart.

Returning to Atlanta, I practically became a one-woman studio turning out films like mad. My Starrbooty epics got the attention of this kid named Wayne Hollowell who was going to the Atlanta College of Art. He was like a modern-day Robert Aldrich of *Whatever Happened to Baby Jane?* fame. He was very exciting to me, because here was someone who had a script, a camera, and the sick sense of humor to go with it. He was an artist, a painter, so he had this beautiful vision of the way things should be. He first came to me with a script called *The Connie Francis Story* in which I was to play the black guy who rapes Connie Francis at the Holiday Inn. But the project that really floated my boat was his script for *Mahogany II*. The title alone was enough to send me to seventh heaven. To play Miss Ross in the sequel! I didn't even have to read the script, I just said, "When do we start?"

In the end the title was perhaps the best thing of all. It has some cute parts. Wayne's films were decidedly more racy, more sexy, more sensationalistic and sicker than anything else I had done before. All his films were laced with gratuitous sex and violence, but it was all done with such humor and lots of ketchup (although later we learned that Hi-C syrup made better blood). The trouble with ketchup was that it made the whole house stink like a garbage dump. But more important than his sophisticated blood techniques was Wayne's enthusiasm, which was so infectious. After *Mahogany II* I starred in *American Porn Star.* My name was firmly above the title—that was always in my contract.

Starrbooty

Then I did *Psycho Bitch* and then, the masterpiece, *Voyeur*. It took four months to film, four whole months, and it's the raciest of them all. I had twenty-two sex scenes with twenty-two tricks. In the end we had to cut them down because there were just too many. To make the film we employed every hustler and transy cruiser within a five-hundred-mile radius as extras. It wasn't too hard to fill those positions. I was the star of Midtown at the time. Everyone knew we were making a movie, and everyone wanted to be in it. Everybody wants to be in a movie, no matter what the budget. Even the dogs on the street were on their hind legs begging for a part.

The story was basically *Basic Instinct* years before it was made, and is about a hooker who kills all her tricks. This guy sees one of the murders by chance, and he falls in love with the

---

FAVORITE TV SHOWS

1. *Style with Elsa Klensch:* Was Gulf War coverage really worth pre-empting Elsa? I don't think so, CNN . . .
2. *Merv:* I wish the show was still around—so I could do it.
3. *The Cher Show:* I never missed an episode.
4. *Mike Douglas:* I grew up with Mike.
5. *Carol Burnett:* My favorite skit was "Blossom Butterworth."
6. *Oprah:* She makes me cry.
7. *Robin Byrd:* When all else fails, Ms. Byrd is always there for you.
8. *The Mary Tyler Moore Show:* Oh, Mr. Grant!
9. *Roseanne:* I love Roseanne so much! What a trooper!
10. *Rhoda:* The funniest ever.
11. *Soul Train:* I watched it religiously in high school.
12. *The Simpsons:* I'm waiting for my cameo, Mr. Groenig.
13. *Melrose Place:* Spelling strikes again.
14. *Martin:* Love it, though I could teach Sheneneh a few tricks of the trade.
15. *Laugh-in:* I'd love to re-create it.
16. *Dynasty:* The classic.
17. *Absolutely Fabulous:* Absolutely fabulous!

---

hooker. He becomes the voyeur of the title and witnesses all the murders. In the climactic scene they finally get it together and, like she's done with all the others, she kills him! In a pool of blood!

For Wayne the fun thing was to audition. He would go out, get drunk, and say, "I'm making a movie, it's full frontal nudity, why don't you audition for me?" The stories he would tell—ah, the power of the casting couch! We had tons of full frontal nudity. At one point I had to take this huge butcher knife and cut off this guy's dick and balls in the shower. This was years before John Wayne Bobbitt. The way it's edited every man watching it goes "Whooo!" when they see the film. You can just taste that knife. As for the boy I was operating on, he must've had a horse for a father.

What can I say, it's a great movie. And let me tell you there's nothing more exciting than having sex on film with a camera crew watching. It's really a big thrill. You act more, you scream more, you writhe more, while making sure that all the time you keep your face toward the camera. I love it.

There's one scene in *Voyeur* that still makes me squirm. It's the scene with me and this black Mandingo stud. We were in this small kitchen, and he mopped the floor with my ass. It was amazing. You can see his big black ass in the camera, and his muscles glistening. Oh child, cool me down.

That said, for the record let me make it perfectly clear that there is *no* penetration in those movies. They are not porno movies, they're comedies. I wouldn't do penetration. Everything was strictly fake. No matter what my booty felt like doing, I stuck to classy Method acting. And I wouldn't do nudity, either. I played a woman, so I always had on at least a bra and a G-string, for tucking. And I always had on a garter belt with stockings and gloves—so I'd be nastier than naked! Sure you'd see the cheeks of my ass, but you'd never set eyes on the crown jewels. Meanwhile, all Wayne ever cared about was the size of my hair. No matter how huge I made it, he'd always say, "No, make it bigger."

I knew when I was making these films that they would resurface when I became a real star. To tell the truth it was a little embarrassing watching some of the films back, 'cause I was playing a whore, cussin' and killin', butt naked and dripping in blood. At the same time being embarrassed was part of my criteria for all the films. Remember this was punk time, and if I didn't feel like, "Oh my God," then I didn't feel that I had done my job. So I'm not ashamed, and if I'm embarrassed, well, that was what punk was all about, being antiestablishment and kicking up a fuss.

Dick, who has always been one of my greatest mentors, always encouraged me. "Just do it," he would always say. The point is, you don't think about waiting for Hollywood to come calling unless you're Meryl Streep . . . and I'm not. You're young now, but this flesh is only flesh and there's an expiration date on it, so you've got to use it and work it and film it while it's young and firm. It's no good trying to be a sex goddess when you're an old and wrinkled prune. My message to all the kids out there is do it now, and then, if you want, you can have a whole lifetime in which to regret it. But I bet you won't. I don't. I am living proof that the do-it-yourself concept works for just about anything. It worked for me, and baby it can work for you too.

Now when I did films with Jon Witherspoon, they premiered at video workshop art houses, and they were written about in art papers. But when I started doing films with Wayne, we had big lavish premieres at Club Rio (the club where Rob Lowe got waylaid by that underage girl). They'd pass out flyers and posters everywhere, "RuPaul is *Mahogany II*" or "RuPaul in *Voyeur.*" On the big night I would arrive in a limousine and get out, and everybody would squeal and scream with flashbulbs popping. We would be whisked to the club's screening room, and afterwards there would be a reception. It was very grand, and I loved it.

All this time—just so I didn't get completely carried away with illusions of grandeur—I was still working as a go-go dancer at Weekends. They also opened up the old movie theater that was adjacent to the club. On weekends they put on drag shows and lipsynching pageants. They made me the official emcee there. I really got to develop my host skills, and learned how to be deliberate. One secret I have learned is that you can never spell it out clear enough. Often I would watch tapes of my performance, and

I could see the places where I needed to take more time. You can never overdo it no matter how slowly you spell out each word. There are all sorts of ways to punch up a situation. Night after night there I made all the mistakes I needed to make, so that later when I got the chance to really emcee in New York, I was already an old hat at it. Weekends was my college years. In fact all of Atlanta was college for me, but at Weekends I was getting paid for my education.

Chapter 11

Down and Out in New York, London, and L.A.

With the harmonic convergence in August '87 things started changing, and I began to feel restless. I knew I had done Atlanta. I'd made a name for myself there, and New York was calling once again. So in the fall Larry Tee, Lahoma, and myself moved up to New York, driving in the Now Explosion's beaten up old van, which was loaded down with all of Lahoma's stuff—films, magazines, books, photography equipment, clothes, pornography . . . There wasn't even room to breathe. All three of us were squeezed into the front seat of the van when suddenly the back tire blew. The van flipped over and spun around on its side. The back door burst open, emptying all Lahoma's belongings onto the highway. None of us were hurt, but we screamed, "Get out!" because we knew that any second an eighteen-wheeler might squish us like bugs. So, we got out and there was stuff everywhere. There were cars stopping and skidding. Dashing among them we gathered up as much stuff as we could, and then limped into a truck stop to calm down. We got towed to some mom-and-pop garage, where they fixed the van and we drove up to New York.

Atlanta's heroes: Me in front of the house where Margaret Mitchell wrote Gone with the Wind.

When that van went over like that, I thought that was it. I thought that I, RuPaul, superstar, had come to the end of the road. On reflection, sitting on the side of the road—Alive!—I saw it as a sign that said, "Your life will never be the same again." We'd had it easy up until then, and this was a new beginning. Atlanta was very safe, and that's why we needed to leave. I knew that I could make money and a name for myself there, but I also knew it was time to go, time to move on. By tipping the van over, the Universe was saying, "Fasten your seat belts, the ride has just begun."

Indeed it had. This was the beginning of a very tough period for me. I got to New York and had to start from the bottom again. We all did. We couldn't get arrested. That's what this business is all about, eating humble pie. It was struggle struggle struggle throughout the year. That Christmas was really hard. New Year's Eve of 1987 I was working coat check at a party at the Amazon Hotel down at Rivington. And I thought here I am, superstar RuPaul, working in coat check! Still, I made sixty dollars. When I did my show at Chameleon—on Sixth and A—I only made eighteen dollars. It was slim pickings for me, very slim.

Larry Tee and Lahoma had moved in with Nelson. I stayed there for a while and then became roommates with my old friend Jennifer, who was working as a go-go dancer and pretty much supporting me. Meanwhile Larry Tee, Lahoma, and I started a night called Disco 88 at the Pyramid. This was the first time I met Michael Alig, and he made my skin crawl. I couldn't believe that Larry Tee and Lahoma took so well to him. But we had to work for him.

Disco 88 was sort of an audition so he could hire us to work for him. And he did hire them, but not me. Disco 88 led to the Celebrity Club at the Tunnel, which was a huge hit.

Your country breakfast is ready.

Some time later I worked for Michael Alig at the Limelight and I rue the day. I had to go to him to get paid, but when I asked for my money he said, "Okay, I'll pay you if you give me a kiss." I said, "Come on, Michael, please, just pay me my money." He said, "Give me a kiss." I couldn't stand him, but I needed to get paid so I said, "Okay, I'll kiss you." I kissed him, and he spat in my

I've done every look in the book.

mouth. It was at that moment that I said to myself "I don't mind doing whatever it takes, but I will never do a fucking thing for you again. Ever. Never ever, ever." So that was that.

In the spring of '88 I went back to Atlanta to act in a play called *Shaggy Dog Animation* by Lee Brewer, with music by Jimmy Harry, and by the same producers who staged *The Rocky Horror Picture Show*. It was quite a difficult stretch. It was about these dogs—actual bow wow wow dogs—who were writing these "Dear John" letters, and explored how men treat women. I got to play a dog. Hell, why not, I've done just about everything else. The show was not a big hit, but the songs were beautiful and I got to meet this fabulous guy called Jimmy. He later told me that he'd seen my posters in Atlanta and said to the director, "This is who you need for this play." I thought, "Hmmm—file him!" and told him if he ever came to New York to look me up so we could work together.

From left to right: Larry Tee, me, and Jon Witherspoon aka Lahoma Van Zant

When the summer was over I moved back to Manhattan. In the meantime Larry Tee and Lahoma had become stars downtown with Michael Alig. I saw that they were changing. The vulnerable part of Larry that I liked wasn't there anymore. You couldn't get through to him. They seemed to be taking on board this whole thing, taking it so seriously. Now I'd been popular before and I knew that ultimately it didn't mean a crock of shit. Not surprisingly, it just wasn't happening for me in New York.

So I went out of the frying pan and into the fire. Scott Lifshutz, a friend, had this one-way ticket to London and asked me if I wanted it. "Sure," I said, thinking that I would go to London and try to make a go of it there. Little did I know what I was letting myself in for. When I get to the other side of the Atlantic, after this hellish overnight flight, they wouldn't let me into the country. They wouldn't let me in because I didn't have a return ticket, no U.K. address, and no money. All I had was Day-Glo nail polish and a Mohawk. And the customs people didn't like that. So they went through every piece of my luggage. Then they stripped me and searched every cavity of my body. Anus, the lot. The only thing they didn't do was spit in my mouth. I think they found one marijuana seed, but that was all they needed to put me back on the plane. I still get the creeps every time I go through customs, particularly in England.

I went back to New York, in dire straits. I thought what I really needed to do was go back to San Diego and recharge my batteries. So I scraped enough money together for a plane ticket to Dallas. It was a flight that went on to San Diego and when it landed I went and hid in the plane's bathroom. Then, over the intercom, the pilot said, "For those of you who are continuing on from Dallas to Atlanta, keep your ticket stubs." I couldn't believe it! The last place I wanted to go was Atlanta. That's what all this was about, leaving Atlanta. So I called my mama from the airport and as luck would have it my sister Renae was in San Antonio, visiting her in-laws. I slept rough in a park in Dallas overnight, and the next day she picked me up. Renae was going back to San Diego, which was where I wanted to go, but first she was going to see my father in Mansfield, Louisiana, which was not where I wanted to go. He had moved back there and opened a beauty supply house. At this point I hadn't spoken to my father in seven years. I was angry with him. But he wasn't fazed. He was like, "Hey buddy," all that. We never dealt with anything. Still, at least I got to see my father's birthplace. Seeing where he came from, was also seeing where I came from ultimately, and so it was good for me.

The next thing I did was move to L.A., to try and make

I've always felt like an observer.

a go of it there. Things were no better. In fact, they were worse. I couldn't get much work. Some people I ran into said *The Gong Show* was back in action, so I went and auditioned, and the next thing I knew I was on. My national television debut was on *The Gong Show*. Things could only go up. I sang "Follow Me" from the Starrbooty album. Salt and Pepa were the judges and at first they looked appalled, but then they got into it. It was quite an experience. I didn't get gonged, but I didn't win either. I lost to an Elvis impersonator.

I stayed all around town. Eventually people got sick of me staying with them. So I went and stayed with my sister Rozy. She got sick of me staying with her too. She said, "Ru, you can't eat any more of the food from my refrigerator or my cupboard." I remember this distinctly because it was the same time that Oprah lost all that weight. She gave me until November 15—just before my twenty-eighth birthday—to get out of the house. Fair enough.

It was a rotten, really rotten time. Because Rozy would go to work at 8:00 A.M. every morning and come home at 5:00 P.M., I'd stay at her house during the day watching television. Then at 4:00 P.M. I would walk to the Beverly Center or Century City Mall and hang out there until she got home and went to bed. That way she wouldn't have to see me, and I wouldn't have to see her. I would sit by the fountains and read discarded newspapers, or spend hours browsing in bookstores. I didn't know anyone, I didn't talk to anyone, it was horrible. I would just wait for the time to pass, minute by minute, hour by hour, until I would walk home again. I've never had any problem day-dreaming, going off into my imagination, but I did during that time. I felt so grounded. I had no car, no money, no friends, and worse than all these things, it seemed like no future. So it was hard just to hide out in myself and play in the realm of my imagination. I had been a star, and now I was on the skids. I'd been trying to make it for seven years and nothing was happening. I couldn't make it in New York, London, or even L.A., the city of the stars. I seriously thought of committing suicide.

There were two things that stopped me. The first thing was knowing that it would hurt my mother, because her philosophy was "Everything will change, so pay it no mind." The other thing was Oprah. I would usually watch her show in one of the department stores at the Beverly Center. In my depths of despair, she was a shining beacon to me, and today I have an Oprah shrine in my home. For a start, she has a quality that can't be learned or knocked off by another person. It's totally her own. People love her

Down and Out ...

because she is totally Oprah; she's herself, she's warm and wears her personality like an old worn coat. She's also someone who is the least likely, according to pop history, to succeed or become a superstar; she was overweight, she's black, and she's a woman with an uncertain background. My heroes are always the underdogs, the people who have made it through adversity to become superheroes—people like Jesus, Buddha, and even Ronald Reagan. Who would have thought this old cowboy could become President once, let alone twice? I didn't agree with his politics for a second— they were appalling—but all the same I couldn't help thinking "That's fierce." I identified with the survivor in him, with the sheer stick-with-it-ness.

Stick-with-it-ness, that's my mantra. And I think it's what got me through, stick-with-it-ness inspired by Oprah and, unlikely as it may sound, Ronald Reagan.

When you turn twenty-eight Saturn returns to the place it was when you were born, which is why that time of life is such a painful

RuPAUL'S FAVORITE BOOKS

1. *Secrets of a Sparrow,* Diana Ross—Now it can be told. The Diva speaks.
2. *Dream Girls: My Life as a Supreme,* Mary Wilson—I love Diana more after reading this book.
3. *Call Her Miss Ross,* J. Randy Traberelli—I love Diana even more after reading this book.
4. *All That Glittered,* Tony Turner—The Supremes behind the scenes, written by their dresser.
5. *I, Tina,* Tina Turner—I read this book when I was on the skids. It gave me strength.
6. *Interview with the Vampire,* Anne Rice—The first book I ever read twice. I fell in love with Louis.
7. *A Return to Love,* Marianne Williamson—The first book I ever read three times. Bought 50 copies for friends and family.
8. *The Color Purple,* Alice Walker—I cried, cried, cried.
9. *Design Your Face,* Way Bandy—This is how I learned to do makeup.
10. *In Cold Blood,* Truman Capote—Very scary, gave me the chills.
11. *The Grass Harp,* Truman Capote—Witness the genius of Truman Capote.
12. *Maybe the Moon,* Armistead Maupin—Sweet story of a freak. Boy, could I relate.
13. *Hitmen,* Fredric Dannen—The record industry inside and out.
14. *Curious George,* H. A. Rey—My first literary obsession.

experience. I equate it with Dorothy going all the way down the yellow brick road, looking behind the curtain, and going, "Is this what I dreamed of? Is that all there is?" You have this splendid vision of the Wiz, and that when you get there everything's going to be great. Then when you get to the Emerald City your life is not transformed, and you have to rethink your expectations and your dreams. That's what I was going through. I had to sit out a couple of years to rethink myself.

But looking back, that period was invaluable because it gave me the strength to know I could go through anything. Once that period passes—as it will—you realize you have muscles of steel, and that nothing can touch you. It is a period that everyone has to go through in their lives, although sadly many people don't make it past that point. Call me a fool, but I really do believe that there is a divine order here, that even all the bad things that happen will have some meaning in the end. Today, when I stay at the penthouse of the Century City Hotel—Hello!—I can't look at the sidewalk without a bittersweet feeling. All that walking!

So I turned twenty-eight and was back out on the street. This was when I finally caved in and surrendered. I decided to go home to Mama for the holidays and just chill out. I quit smoking, gained twenty-five pounds, and grew a beard for the first time in my life. I spent a lot of time with my niece Morgan, who was eleven years old and the only person I could really talk to.

Chapter 12

Queen of Manhattan

With the new year came new energy. From time to time while I was away I would talk to Larry Tee, who would say, "Ru, get on a plane and come back to New York. I'll give you the money whenever you want it. Just come back." Finally, I got over myself and decided that I would "do" New York just like I had "done" the Breakfast Club all those years ago. I said to myself, "I am going to work this motherfucker into a frenzy!" I took him up on his offer, told him I'd pay him back with three days of go-go dancing, and got a one-way ticket.

When I came back to New York in January of '89 the call was for drag queen realness—tits, the lot. Undeterred I said to myself, "I'm a fiercer drag queen than any of these queens, I'm a sexier drag queen than any of these queens, I'm a prettier drag queen than any of these queens, and I'm a better emcee than any of these queens." If that was what the children wanted, then that was what the monster would serve them.

RuPaul takes a bite out of the big apple.

I moved in with Larry Tee and Lahoma at Nelson's house and started working it in a big way, really doing it right. I learned how to lipsynch—not just approximately, but with laser precision. I began buying wigs—I had never done that before—started sewing clothes, wearing tits, and shaving my legs. Instead of fright drag, I was going to look hot and sexy as a drag queen.

Suzanne Bartsch started using me as a go-go dancer at Sauvage for fifty bucks a night. I was up to my old tricks. I didn't just prance on a box, I was a show. She thought I was a new kid on the block and didn't know that I had go-go danced my way right out the womb. She came over later and said, "Girl you got it going on. You have the ability to be a real pop star, you have what it takes." Unlike some other club promoters, she always treated me with

The crowning of the King (Kenny Kenny) and
Queen of Manhattan.

respect and always pushed me to do more, like emceeing. She didn't pay a lot of money, but she always respected my talent, and for that I will be forever grateful.

That summer it was Love Machine that really put us over the top. After the success of the Celebrity Club this was Larry Tee's own operation in what had been the old Underground Club. Finally we—Lady Bunny, Floydd, Lahoma, and I—all had a home, and were back under one roof just like we were down South. We all had a place where we could all go to work, get drunk, and become stars. It was a really dark time in New York, and the Love Machine was just what people were looking for. What with the election of Bush, AIDS, and deepening recession, people had just about had it up to here with doom and gloom. We put life back into New York. We were the new drag queens—the Charlie's Angels of downtown—smart, sassy, cynical but loving, approachable, and with a sense of humor. If you asked a question, we weren't going to bite your head off like some of the other evil queens. It was, "Hey, come on down, y'all." As a Miss Black America finalist, I knew how to work that thing. I don't do bitchy. I do sassy. I had been doing "Everybody say love" since Lord knows when. So when I came on the scene with this love message coming from a drag queen that wasn't, "Bitch! You better get your ass outta my face—" it made an instant connection. Us southern belles were a breath of fresh air. We merged the southern realness thing with the ratty old wigs and social satire of the Pyramid. We brought a new freedom that totally liberated and reinvented drag.

I had a deal with the Love Machine. Larry would pay me a hundred bucks a week and I could do whatever I wanted: lipsynch a number, emcee, tell jokes—whatever. One of my favorite things to do were the Champale commercials. Champale—for those of you who don't know—is a pink-colored combination of beer and champagne.

The drink was vile, but the commercials were the best. They ran on the black stations and it would consist

Her royal highness.

of this woman talking about Champale occasions. They
went something like this:

> Ladies, I want to talk to you about Champale occasions.
> You know, those special occasions where you just have *got*
> to celebrate with sparkling Champale? What if a prince
> comes up to you driving a Rolls-Royce and asks you to go
> to his private island via his Lear jet? Now you'd celebrate
> that with sparkling Champale, wouldn't you? Okay, what if
> a duke comes up to you in a Lincoln Town Car and you both

fly first class to his beach house? Now you'd celebrate that with sparkling Champale, wouldn't you? Okay, now what if a guy comes up to you with a dog named Duke, two bus tokens, and you both take the train to look at other people's beach houses? You'd celebrate that with sparkling Champale, wouldn't you?

I would just get up on stage, fueled with a few cocktails, and recite those ads word for word and the audience loved it. It just goes to show it's not *what* you say, but *how* you say it that counts.

The success with Champale inspired me to launch my own fragrance and do my own line of commercials. The perfume wars at the time were fierce. Liz Taylor was ruling the market with Passion. Forever Crystal, Linda Evans's *Dynasty* fragrance, was flagging, and Joan Collins was having mixed success trying to give Scoundrel away. I decided to launch a fragrance that said it all and spelled it out quite clearly. It was called Whore, For She Who Is. Reediting scenes from my previous movies, I made a whole series of commercials and recorded a bunch of jingles to go with them.

Normally at the Love Machine I would kick off my show with a Whore or Champale commercial, throw in a quick "Everybody say love"—maybe even get the whole audience chanting "ohhhhmmmmmm" in an effort to be "at one"—and then finish it all off by lipsynching a number. My most famous lipsynching number was "If I Could Turn Back Time" by Cher. No one else was doing that. My look was very black hooker, very foxy lady. I would do rock and disco numbers like "Hot Stuff" by Donna Summer, and "Do You Want to Touch Me" by Joan Jett.

Now I can reveal the secrets to lipsynching. Now it can be told. First, not all songs are drag-friendly. As with so many things in life, the choice is the thing! It had to have that southern perspective; it either had to be funny or have a certain irony that came from seeing a drag queen perform it. When I heard the queens were doing supermodel in the South, it was the ultimate compliment. I really knew I had made it then.

Queen of Manhattan

Then you have to practice that mother over and over. But you don't—and this may seem surprising to some people—have to know all the words. You have to *live* the song, every breath and every beat. Beyond that it doesn't really matter if you know the words or not. People are not looking at your mouth to check you've got the words right, they're drinking in the whole picture—the gestures, the moves, the attitude. If the attitude is right, the words are the last thing you need. It's really all about Method acting. A lot of times the girls lipsynch and have all the words, but they are not connecting with the song or with the audience. Well, you could be reading the Declaration of Independence, but if you're not making that connection, all the words in the world aren't going to make the difference.

It's total Kabuki. It's all about exaggerating your face and body movements, where your every gesture tells a story. When it came to telling a story, the girls down South were totally over the top and an inspiration. There was Chocolate

BEST RECORDS TO LIPSYNCH

(Don't do slow songs unless you're a pro.)
1. Cher: **"Save Up All Your Tears;" "If I Could Turn Back Time"**
2. Joan Jett: **"Do You Wanna Touch Me;" "I Hate Myself for Loving You"**
3. Taylor Dayne: **"I'll Be Your Shelter;"** "Every Beat of My Heart;" "Prove Your Love;" "I'll Wait"
4. Donna Summer: **"Hot Stuff;"** "On the Radio;" **"This Time I Know It's for Real"**
5. Whitney Houston: **"So Emotional;"** "Dance with Somebody;" "How Will I Know"
6. Michele: "No More Lies"
7. Jennifer Holliday: "No Frills Love"
8. Patti LaBelle: "Right Kind of Lover;" "Think about You"
9. Melba Moore: "Lean on Me"
10. Jody Watley: **"Some Kinda Love;"** "Don't You Want Me;" **"Most of All;" "Real Love;"** "Everything;" "Heaven Must Be Missing an Angel"
11. Gloria Gaynor: **"I Will Survive"**
12. Tina Turner: "What You Get Is What You See"
13. Boycrazy: "That's What Love Can Do"
14. Vanessa Williams: "Running Back to You"
15. Natalie Cole: "Party Lights (Live)"
16. Aretha Franklin: "Another Night"
17. Eurythmics: "Would I Lie to You;" "Must Be Missing an Angel"
18. Nicole: **"Don't You Want My Love"** (*Ruthless People* soundtrack)
(Selections in bold are my personal favorites.)

Thunderpussy who was no waif—she was a big-boned girl. Couple of hundred pounds. But that didn't stop her from doing a triple somersault in six-inch heels across the stage at the climax of "Who's Zooming Who" by Aretha Franklin. If I'm lying I'm flying, and you don't see no wings.

Another popular thing down South is the rubber face, where you make your mouth do one thing and your eyes do another. That's as basic to lipsynching as bricks to buildings. One of my favorite moves—and you can do this at home too—is to lick your finger, as if you had just dipped it in honey, and then trace a spiral circle on the wall. Then quickly slap the wall—pow!—as if you're smacking a roach. It can really help you get your point across.

And let me tell you, the Lady Bunny is the most incredible lipsynch artist out there. She's a great mimic. I'll never forget her rendition of "Popcorn" by Hot Butter. She got all those pom pom pom pom pom pom poms smack dab on. It was a sight that could make a drag queen cry. Back down in Atlanta, when we were inseparable, we would go out and clock the moves of all the drag queens. I have a different style from her, but we're from the same source, with plenty of bubbles for whatever you fancy.

The second week of the Love Machine was Independence Day, but Nelson died of a heart attack in the early hours of that morning, which cast a dark cloud over everything. That night we had all been having a party in Nelson's backyard, making hamburgers. Around midnight I left. I meant to say goodbye, to give him a hug and a kiss, but a lot of people were there, and he was washing dishes from the meal, so I thought I would just wait. *Never* wait to tell someone or show them that you love them. Trade called me at two that morning with the news. I couldn't believe it. We had become very close when things had been really tough for me. It was the first time someone who I was really close to, who I saw every day, died. I only really came into my own after he died—and I'm sorry he never saw that.

That was the only thing to mar the experience of the

Love Machine, which instantly became *the* party in town, and the A-list flocked. I remember Liza Minnelli going there when her album was out and heading for the DJ booth and asking, "Do you guys have my new single?" which, if I remember rightly, was the camp classic "Losing My Mind." They didn't have it, but Larry Tee played the Pet Shop Boys instead.

The Love Machine was a springboard to a whole host of other things. All of a sudden we were the new darlings of downtown, and the offers started pouring in. Suzanne Bartsch started asking me to emcee for her at Copacabana, which was another A-list event. Then the B-52s asked me to be in their *Love Shack* video. *Love Shack* was a big hit and still plays on VH-1. Then in January 1990 I was crowned Queen of Manhattan. I was the first black queen to wear that crown, and also the first queen of the nineties, a truly new age.

Only a year ago I had been sitting all by my lonesome in the Beverly Center, thinking of cashing in my dance card and hustling to that great boogie wonderland in the sky. Now I know that a lot of people don't take "Queen of Manhattan" seriously, and of course you shouldn't, but I was not going to take it for granted. I milked that sucker for all it was worth. I reigned all that year like a queen should. I had pictures made up that said "Queen of Manhattan 1990," I really did! Even today the other queens don't really take it to town. But I did. I used it as a launch pad.

During my reign *Geraldo* was a high point. At first he wanted me in the audience, but I said, "I ain't getting out of bed unless I'm on the panel." So the word came back that they needed a black person on the panel because they didn't have one to represent the club scene, which was basically all white—and that ain't no lie.

The episode was to be called "The Agony and the Ecstasy," and was to be all about drugs on the scene. Geraldo had his agenda. He wanted a tabloid show about all these wild kids running around New York whacked out on drugs. But I had my own agenda. I still felt like I was biding my time, and although I didn't know exactly what it

was, I knew I had more to offer than "Hey, y'all." This was my opportunity to show that I was more than just the Queen of Manhattan. And television—a language I have always spoken fluently—was my way of taking it to another level. Because we were on such a gutter tabloid level, it really wasn't difficult to out pooh the pooh.

I didn't plan to upstage the others, but everyone was so well behaved. I always forget that people get nervous and can't talk on TV. I have never had that problem! Doing *The American Music Show* every week for years and years and years and years, I already had a TV career before I even came to New York. And the one thing I have learned is that a camera is a camera is a camera, and they demand a certain performance. It's like feeding a lion. If you go up to the cage shaking and say, "Here's your food, Mr. Lion," the lion will bite your arm off. But if you march right up to that sucker and say, "Here's your meat, now eat it!" the lion can only obey you (kids, do not try this when you go the zoo!). It's really no different with the camera. The camera loves the people who love it.

On the set of the B52's Love Shack *video.*

During the taping of the *Geraldo* show, I said there was more to clubbing than just kids dressing up. It was a sign of people being free spirits. I said, "These bodies, this flesh and blood, they too are drag, because they are just temporary outfits for our eternal souls, Amen." At another point I yelled out, "Everybody put your hands on your TV set, because this is the most important thing you'll ever hear." It may have been the Ecstasy, but I could feel the whole nation leap up from their sofas and place their hands on top of mine on the television screen.

"Now everybody say love!" I said.

"Love!" everyone roared in the audience.

"*Everybody* say love!"

"Love!" roared the entire nation with one accord.

And then the kicker . . .

"'Cause if you can't love yourself—how in the hell you gonna love somebody else—can I get an A-men in here?"

It was fun—but it was also true.

Anyone with a heart who was watching could see that here were young people being free. Instead of seeing life in black and white—and maybe a bit of gray—they were indiscriminately using all the colors of the rainbow in their palette. That's what the club kids are all about: dressing up and having fun. That's what we're here for. In the animal kingdom that's what the male of the species does in his natural state, he struts about like a peacock. So for me to be in drag using all these colors, and for all these kids to be using glitter and what have you, that's what it's all about. The medium is the message, and no matter what moralistic, judgmental frame Geraldo tried to put the whole thing in, I think my point came across. And a lot of people in the audience, on the panel, and at home watching sat up and took notice: "Here's a live one. She's definitely got something else going on." They got to see that I was more than just a fierce drag queen. Something *I* knew all along!

That show was also the first time my mother saw me in full female drag. I was wearing a necklace that she had given me—a piece of bad seventies costume jewelry, but she didn't notice that. All she said was, "Why are you wearing *all* that makeup? That's too much makeup." And you know what? She was absolutely right!

In spite of all this fabulousness that was going on, it

wasn't all sunny and cher. By this point I really had a drinking problem. Lahoma and I at this time were drinking like fiends. Drinking wasn't all bad, because it provided an opportunity for some of my alter egos to surface. Bianca Dinkins was my drunk persona. She was who I turned into at two in the morning after eight cocktails. Bianca was the illegitimate daughter of David Dinkins, "whose father threw her out of the house 'cause she stole her daddy's color TV set. Now, what kind of way is that to treat your daughter, can you answer me that?" The alcohol certainly seemed to fuel the characters, which in turn fueled the audience.

But then it was getting to the point where I needed a real cocktail—three-quarters vodka and a quarter-inch of orange juice—just to get me started. I was at the latter part of my go-go career, and it wasn't interesting to me anymore. I wasn't getting any younger—but the kids were—and I needed something a little more than coffee to get me through the night. I felt old. I didn't feel that I belonged, and I didn't understand why I was doing it anymore. So to get excited about it, I had to have a drink. Several drinks.

Meanwhile, in my zonked out way I was trying to get a singing career together. Larry Tee and I started working on a song for Cardiac Records. It was called "I Got That Feeling," which really meant "I Don't Got That Feeling," because I was so tanked up on booze and drugs I couldn't feel a thing. More than that Larry Tee wasn't hearing what I was saying, and I wasn't hearing what he was saying. It was a mess. Somehow we got that song recorded.

And then there was the Robert Palmer video fiasco.

They were shooting the video right outside the door of Nelson's house, where we all were living. The Lower West Side of Manhattan, more popularly known as the Meat Packing District, had become très trendy since they shot *Fatal Attraction* there, and it was the place for many *Vogue* fashion shoots. One day I staggered in at some ungodly hour and the street was full of supermodels. Linda, Christie, and Naomi were sitting on the steps of Nelson's house. At first I thought it was the drugs, and then I

Lettin It All Hang Out

thought I was having a vision. But once I started chatting with them they seemed real enough. Turns out they were doing a massive photo shoot for Chanel. Quite a bizarre combination, haute haute couture in this grimy low-rent district. Once that spread came out, the fashion world and its dog wanted to do something there. Robert Palmer, who had made his mark in music videos by packing them with hundreds of ice-cool model clones, was obviously not going to be left out. So one day I staggered in from a full night out and there were all these cranes,

Me and Lahoma on the set of the Robert Palmer video.

cameras, and lights in the street. It looked like a full-fledged feature shoot.

In no time we got cast. They had a holding pen for all the extras, and we were waiting there ready to go on. We had a gallon of vodka with us and someone offered us a Quaalude. Just as it was beginning to kick in, we were called to get ready to go on. The last thing I remember was riding the elevator to wardrobe . . .

The next morning I woke up lying on the couch with the TV going, still in drag and with my makeup on. I had no idea how I got there. Since it was a two-day shoot, I headed back to the set in the evening.

But when we got there, they told us we were not working.

"Oh yes we are," I said.

Then they told us that we'd been fired the night before for being so fucked up and out of control. I must have still been high, because I then had the nerve to kick up such a big stink that they said we could work after all, which just meant hanging around all night and getting paid for it. They didn't film us.

When the video finally came out, there I was prancing around, having a conversation with Robert Palmer, dropping my purse, having him pick it all up, and I could not remember any of it. Not a single thing.

I had finally gone overboard. I'd been fired from a gig for being sauced! That's when I said to myself, "This has got to stop, I can't go to work fucked up on liquor and Quaaludes." The big thing I remember from the School of Performing Arts is that you need to show up and be a professional. Broadway doesn't stand for booze and pills.

It was time to clean house and move on.

13

Chapter

Work the Runway, Sweetie

I did a trip with Suzanne Bartsch to Miami in December 1990. I went to this Ford Model Agency party, had about ten cocktails, but felt nothing. To tell you the truth I was scared. I was scared that I had turned thirty in November and seemed to have so little to show for it. I was scared that the little I did have—my reign as

Urban Cowboy

Queen of Manhattan—was coming to an end. I was scared that I couldn't leave the house to go work in a club without a cocktail or three. I was scared that a dozen cocktails later I still didn't get a buzz. And I was scared thinking, "Where am I gonna take it from here, what am I gonna do for an encore?"

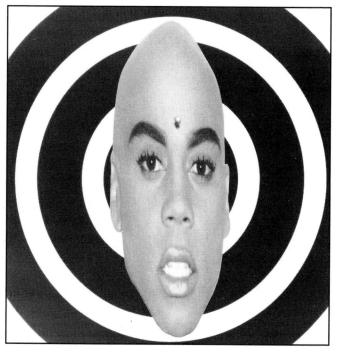

On the other hand, I'd made it to thirty in the fast lane, and so it was not a fluke I was still around. I decided that from now on I would be here for this life, and that I would be there for me. I quit drinking, quit doing drugs, and I started to take care of myself, getting up in the morning and going to aerobics classes. I still continued to smoke pot, but I cut out caffeine and all other narcotics. And once I had made *that* decision, the fear melted away. I wasn't scared anymore. I didn't know what lay ahead, but whatever it was I was doing the right thing, so I knew that one way or another I would make it.

My life changed totally. For one thing, it was the first time I really saw New York. Although I'd been there for years, it was the first time I saw the city by day, knew what streets were what, and learned where things were. Until then I didn't know the West Village from the East Village, because I'd normally be in a drunken stupor and see it whizzing by from inside a cab. When I was doing the clubs I slept all day and woke up in the evening with just enough time to get something to eat, take a shower, get in drag, have a cocktail, and go out. You had to go out every night to get the go-go gigs, and if you were gone for more than a week "they" wouldn't know if you still had the juice to go over big at "their" party. Out of sight was out of mind. So you had to go out. It was a treadmill. I was, I suppose, a real slave of New York. But once I quit night life I became a student of New York. I would get up, put on

I thought I couldn't make it as a star if I did drag. Instead I worked an androgynous look.

my backpack, and go do my work, which involved a lot of footwork. I had to walk around all day because I didn't have money to catch cabs, and I was living off popcorn and seltzer from the Film Forum theater where my friend Floydd worked.

World of Wonder was the production company started by the Pop Tarts. I knew that their pop dreams had crashed and burned thanks to a couple of rotten record contracts. But at least they had gotten the record contracts in the first place. They had also notched up a couple of publishing deals and had gotten disco diva Dan Hartman to produce their record. So, thinking that there might be something for me there, I started sounding them out about management, and soon we had an agreement in place.

I knew it was a new chapter of my story, because I was around people who were making it happen on a real level and not on a bullshit level, drunk in a club saying, "I'm writing a screenplay and I'm gonna fly to the moon tomorrow." World of Wonder was a place where it actually happened: "We shoot next week, you gotta be there at such and such a time." With World of Wonder, it was the first time I was sober, ready to work, and I felt like it was a chance for me to really make it.

The hardest thing of all was that in the course of getting sober I inevitably distanced myself from all the people and the places I was hanging out with. I had to do it, but they weren't having any of it. Maybe they felt abandoned, betrayed. Maybe they felt threatened when they saw that I was really trying to make a career for myself and go for it with my music. "Oooh, child, who she think she is? She thinks she's the passionate one." And so when I changed my life in a positive way, maybe that sent a message to some of my friends loud and clear that it was probably time for them to clean up their act too. Of course, people generally don't like wake-up calls. No one likes to get out of bed in the morning until they're good and ready, and even then it may not be a pretty sight. I had already had my wake-up call with the fact that the life I was leading and the stuff I was doing just wasn't working. There was also the success of Deee-Lite. When they made it, I was like, "Hey—they were supposed to make it *after* I made it." I admired them, but in my mind I was before them in the queue for international stardom. Unless I got my act together I was going to miss my turn—and there was no way in hell I was going to let that happen.

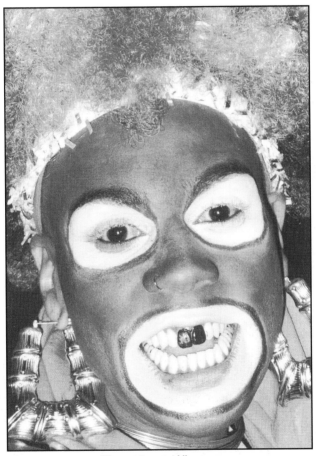

Glamour is my middle name.

Skipping the drugs and the drink was easy, but having no friends—that was the hardest part. I felt like a divorced wife. Mind you, there wasn't anything I could do except ride it out. I had been in that exact same situation before. When I was a kid in San Diego, I'd go to the beach. When I got back home the kids would say, "What are you doing going to the beach? You must think you white or something." People in my neighborhood didn't go to the beach, it wasn't ours. But there I was venturing outside of my area to do something different—something I've done my whole life.

For the first time in my life I made a real effort at making it happen. I'd always taken my creativity for granted, really. I'd always subconsciously thought, "This is mine," but now I made a concentrated effort on really making it happen. I figured I had enough time to invest a year in something and make it really good, and so just after the new year I started writing songs with Jimmy. The first song we wrote was "Under the Influence of Love," and the second was "Prisoner of Love"— the song that ultimately got me my record contract.

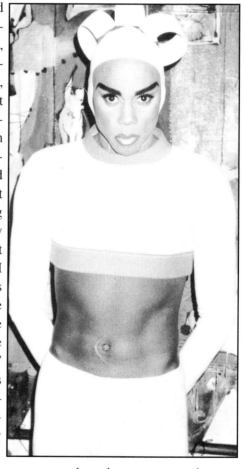

Meanwhile, I was supposed to be out promoting Larry's record, "I Got That Feeling," but the record wasn't doing much. When I did track dates I was wearing a hot pink bodysuit with tight-fitting hood and matching ostrich trim. I looked like Gumby on a Pepto-Bismol diet. After the shows people would say, "That's great, but what's happening with Starrbooty? What's happening with your drag career?" At that point I felt that if I was ever going to become a star, I'd have to be androgynous or whatever.

Anything but a drag queen. I wasn't fighting it, but I did think that beyond an underground downtown audience, drag simply wouldn't translate. I had no idea that what worked at the Pyramid would work just as well in a massive stadium, or in a Hollywood movie. With the exception

of Divine and Sylvester, no one had carried it off, and even then, for all their groundbreaking success, they seemed to make it only so far. Sure, I'd done my movies in drag, but I never thought of presenting myself as *the* premier drag queen for mass consumption, for the MTV kids who go to the mall.

But that was the message people were sending me, and then suddenly it clicked. I thought to myself, You know, these people *want* to see you in drag. I know in retrospect it must seem like, "Duh," but so often the most obvious things, the things that everybody else can see, are the ones that we have the hardest time seeing ourselves. I looked around at my favorite stars and realized that they were drag queens too. In fact *every* celebrity is a drag queen. They put on glamourous personas and masks for their audience. At the same time I realized that there wasn't an out and out drag queen who is a total star. So why not just take it over the top completely? Why not just pump glamour to the hun-

dredth degree? And why not have the most unlikely person of all do it—a big old black man? I
thought people could get off on that. So I said to myself,
"I'm going to wear the longest legs, the highest shoes, the
shortest hot pants, the biggest hair, and . . . show as many
teeth as possible."

A supermodel was born!

And so you see I had to go all around the block to find
out that what I should be doing was right there for me all
along. Très Oz.

Ever since the day I made that decision, everything fell
into place. Well, almost.

I continued to spend a lot of time at World of Wonder:
They were sending out my demo tapes and producing a late
night series called "Manhattan Cable" for British TV.
While we waited for the deal offers to pour in, I made some
cash money by doing some roving reports on the streets of
Manhattan: interviewing the Rockettes and doing a segment on the new black Barbie doll, Shani. But my first
assignment was transvestite hookers.

Manhattan's transvestite hookers hung out on the
streets where I lived, virtually next door to the Anvil and
the Vault, two sex clubs. They were a nice bunch of girls
catering to the bridge and tunnel crowd, straight men who
would come in from New Jersey looking for the girl with
something extra—about twelve inches extra. I got to know
many of them and found that I identified with them very
strongly. In fact, I felt that in terms of what I was doing and
what I wanted to do, I was one of them. When I was doing
Queen of Manhattan, I was basically a classy hooker—sort
of. I had to schmooze people, I had to put out for people.
People I didn't necessarily like. And what is a pop star
other than a hooker? When I finally got the hit record I was
dreaming of, I wasn't actually going to sell myself body
and soul, but the more I thought about it, that was exactly
what I was going to have to do: I was going to have to sell
my ass in every way possible—in print, on video, on television, on radio—whore myself for the sake of the record.
I was going to have to bow and scrape and kiss ass to a

bunch of assholes, so, really, what was the difference? They were doing the same thing, except that it was much more direct, much more honest. Hookers—transsexual or otherwise—really are the unsung heroes of our society. Although they are spurned and treated like trash, they have tremendous power, and I have nothing but awe and admiration for them.

I'd never actually been one per se, although I have had a couple of experiences. Once, after getting off work at the Red Zone on Fifty-fourth Street, I hailed a cab to take me to the World, down on the Lower East Side. As luck would have it, the driver was a foot worshipper. As I got in he said that if I would put my foot over the seat while he jacked off he would give me the cab ride for free. For a career girl working in the city on a fixed budget I was never going to pass up the opportunity to save a

The return of Starrbooty

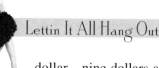

dollar—nine dollars and fifty cents to be exact—
although it took a little longer to reach my desti-
nation.

To do my assignment I decided it would be a good
idea for me to go "undercover," and disguise myself as one
of them—what a stretch of the imagination. Somehow I
managed to pull together an appropriate outfit, and a few
hours after midnight on a sultry summer night, we hit the
streets. In search of meat.

First we began with some general shots of my pound-
ing the streets working the look and feel of a whore. Then
we decided to get some interviews. I would run up to the
girls, explain what we were doing, and ask them if I could
interview them. Once I had managed to persuade them to
speak to us (and get a signed release), I waved the camera
crew over. We got a lot of great stuff. I mean, come on, a
bunch of drag queens and a camera crew, what more could
you ask for? After we got a bunch of good sound bites,
including a pretty in-depth description of a famous male

comic who enjoyed
boy/girls, all we
needed was a sexy
ending to the story.

"Why not," I
suggested, "get a
shot of me ap-
proaching a car as a
hooker?" Seemed
the obvious thing to
do, really. As the
cameraman and crew
ran across Four-
teenth Street, I
positioned myself
in the middle of the
intersection. A black
car came cruising
up the street, and it
slowed down right

alongside of me. This was perfect. I couldn't resist taking it further, and decided to get him to roll down his window and engage in a little chitchat. So I bent down, positioning myself so that I wouldn't block the window from the camera. Sure enough the guy rolls down his window just as I had planned. What I didn't plan was that this guy was the most gorgeous man I had seen in a lifetime. He was a corrections officer. Twenty-three years old, from Yonkers, New York. Hot Italian—mama mia, what a spicy meatball. Totally KFC. He began rubbing his crotch.

I explained that I was a reporter for British TV doing a story on transvestite hookers and that we were filming the final shot. He didn't believe me—who would? As I was trying to point out the camera crew, he was telling me that my legs were gorgeous, and that if I were a thorough reporter I would get in the car and do some in-depth investigation. Of course I resisted. After all, I was a journalist not a hooker. But, trust me, this man was a god—an Italian stallion. Then he said that a good reporter wouldn't pass up a lead like this, and he started to unzip . . .

By now the camera crew must have got more than enough material, but I started thinking to myself, "Gee, if I get into the car and it drives off, now wouldn't *that* be the perfect ending to my report?" I grabbed the door handle and hopped into the car, sacrificing myself for the story, like any good journalist.

On location in Gallipoli, Italy, for Ellen Von Untwerth's film **Inferno.**

As we drove off, the camera crew walked into the center of the street and then, when the car did not stop and I did not get out, they started running after the car. Meanwhile, I had my hands full with the driver.

It was a quick ride around the block, although the camera crew didn't think so. When I finally got back, I bought them all breakfast with the thirty-five-dollar bonus I had just earned, so they weren't too upset. To this day it cracks me up to think that my debut on national British television as a reporter ends with me turning a trick.

A few weeks later the phone rang. My demo tape had landed on the desk of Monica Lynch, the president of Tommy Boy records. Within moments of listening to the tape she had picked up the phone and announced her intention of signing me to the label. I was stunned. Tommy Boy was, after all, a hard-core rap label; what could they want with a big black drag queen?

The negotiations went on for the requisite number of months, and during that time Wigstock swung around. Wigstock is the drag queen version of Woodstock. It is an annual all-day downtown extravaganza held every Labor Day weekend, hosted by its founder the "Lady" Bunny. All

Me and my true-blue friend P.J.

the drag queens get together in Tompkins Square Park in the East Village, and later at the Christopher Street pier once it outgrew the park, for a festival of peace, love, and hair grease. My first Wigstock had been in 1989 when I did Whitney, "So Emotional" before a medium-sized crowd. But in the intervening years the festival had grown into quite an extravaganza attended by drag queens from all over the country and all over the world. The crowds had grown to tens of thousands, with dozens of news crews from CNN to the BBC hovering in the wings. Wigstock 1991 would prove to be a particularly important gig for me because Monica from Tommy Boy announced that she was going to come down and check me out.

Now the day before that particular Wigstock I moved out of Nelson's old place, where I had been living for the past year with Lahoma and Larry Tee, into an apartment with my new friend P.J. on Fifth Street and Avenue C. When Nelson died the whole downstairs of his three-story house was a warehouse of stuff from twelve years of junk collecting. Boxes and boxes of stuff. I had moved in there and made a home for myself. I went through the boxes of stuff he had left behind, stuff that no one wanted. Some I kept—like an old stereo—and most I gave away. I gave things to everybody: tripods, ties, shoes. Then, when I finally moved out, I brought this air conditioner with me that I found under the stairs. I suppose I shouldn't have taken it—but no one had been using it when I found it. I didn't think that I was stealing it, but that was the word that went around, that I had stolen their air conditioner.

But it wasn't really about the air conditioner, no one cared two cents about that old thing. What they cared about was someone stepping out on their own, taking control of their life. Whenever that happens it's always the same old story: "Oh, you think you're too good for us." The air conditioner was just the lightning rod for everyone's pent-up resentment.

Because there I was, at Wigstock on Labor Day 1991, waiting to go on stage, knowing that so much hung on my performance. But waiting backstage to go on and do my number no one said a word to me. Not one. Not even the stage manager who was normally in my face about his poetry readings. And so that I could be in no doubt about the hostile vibes I was being sent, seconds before I went on Jack, my old heart throb, spoke up and said, in true Ru monster tradition, "Everybody say 'Thief!'" in a cruel parody of my trademark saying, "Everybody say 'Love.'"

"What?" I said. I simply could not believe that I had heard what I thought I had heard.

Me and the "Lady" Bunny.

Like the kids calling me a sissy all those years back, he was not shy about saying the same thing twice.

"Everybody say 'Thief!'" he hollered.

It really took me aback. But there was no time. Suddenly I heard my name being announced on stage, and as I stepped out to the opening bars of "Everybody Say 'Love,'" I remembered thinking, "I'm gonna show these motherfuckers!" And that's what I did, even though Jack's remark was still ringing in my ears.

I was featuring a prototype supermodel

look—some glamour but still the hooker. A cheap, cheap, cheap, red sequined dress, a big blond Ivana Trump updo, and huge black and white op art earrings. For the show I changed into a shiny black plastic raincoat, which I removed at the beginning of my second number to reveal a white bathing suit with a waist cincher that was cutting me in half like a pair of scissors (no pain, no gain is always the golden rule).

Coming off stage it was just as icy. No one had a word to say. Fortunately, I had my posse there, my new buddy P.J. and his friends. But I didn't have too much time after the show to stew in my own juice, because we were all selling T-shirts. I learned early on that you make your money in concessions, not ticket sales. Even as a little bitty drag queen I knew it was all about merchandising. I sold the postcards, my books, T-shirts. It's all for sale, baby, we're all born to be sold. That's what pop culture is—one big marketplace. If you're gonna be out there signing autographs, why not make it something that you can sell? I stood outside the backstage area hawking them until they were all gone. Appropriately, the slogan on the shirts was "Everybody Say 'Love.'"

At the end of the day I knew that I was on my way to getting beyond all of the high school politics—at least that particular high school, the nightclub scene, where "high" is an operative word. High school prepares you for the rest of your life because if you can survive that, you can survive anything. Like I've always said, life is no different from high school: the cliques, the politics, the petty jealousies— it's just the same old shit in a different wrapper, that's all. Although I hadn't done anything wrong, I brought the air conditioner back.

Most of the people who snubbed me at Wigstock have since come back to me and said, "You were fierce and fearless, we knew you were going to make it all along." Although they couldn't bring themselves to say it at the time, they really did believe I was going to make it. They knew it, I knew it, we all knew it. And their support and that energy—however it was expressed—really did help put me where I am today.

Although Starrbooty had always been a fashion model turned secret agent, Larry Tee noticed how in recent months I had been working the glamourous supermodel aspect of the character. He called me up and suggested I do a prequel to that story, and call it *Supermodel*. I was wary at first because of all we had been through in the past. But a good idea is a good idea, and this time he was right on it. My writing partner Jimmy Harry and I took that and wrote *Supermodel*. My favorite line is rhyming "savoir faire" with "million dollar derriere."

When we were done, we knew we had tapped into the Zeitgeist. It was just at that time that Naomi, Linda, Christie, and Co. were being worshipped as superstars with the adoration normally reserved for rock gods. I think that it had all to do with the death of the great stars of the silver screen. Think about it, there aren't anymore really glamourous film stars. Today's female stars are working women, or else the love interest of male gods like Schwarzenegger and all the other action heroes—that is where the focus is in movies. The mantle of glamour has been taken from the women and given to the men. The women toil in their shadows, plain and ordinary-looking. So that transition has left a void. It is a void for drop-dead, impossible, over-the-top glamour. Supermodels fill that void. The only thing they have to do is work the runway, sweetie, and refuse to get out of bed for less than ten thousand dollars. As they sashay down the narrow strip, they don't have to say anything, because words are superfluous when you're working the pure essence of glamour. It's p o w e r f u l stuff, and we all need a little bit of undiluted glamour in our lives.

So in *Supermodel*

*Blond hair on brown skin is
a visual blitz.*

we put in a little rap breakdown where I name check the famous models, saying that they are the heirs to the glamour of old Hollywood. But we also did an alternate mix, where I name the leading drag queens: The "Lady" Bunny, Lahoma, Tabboo, Mona Foot, Zaldy, Princess Diandra. That's because the drag queen and the supermodel are in my mind almost one and the same. If you were to see a supermodel out of her drag

You can call me "he," you can call me "she," you can call me "Regis and Kathie Lee."

you wouldn't recognize her. Some of the most unforgettable women in the world are men, like Billy Beyond, who walks in all the Todd Oldham shows, Connie Girl for Thierry Mugler, and Lypsinka for Gaultier. The point is that drag is pure glamour too. It's all about playing with the essence, and that's why drag queens have become so popular recently. These girls—like the fabulous Candis Cayne, Mistress Formika, Kabuki Starshine, Girlina and Afrodite, for example— looked like they came right out of the pages of any fashion magazine. They are fierce. They're not really a parody of women, and they can really hold their own in a roomful of supermodels any day. The only difference is that unlike the supermodels, these girls will get out of bed for a lot less than ten thousand dollars. They are working girls. The new queen sings, dances, does her own makeup, her own hair, and styles herself. She makes her own clothes, she dresses up-to-date, and keeps up with the trends. They work hard for the money.

Originally the album was going to be called *Starrbooty,* but then as the supermodel concept took hold of my imagination, there was nothing else to call it other than *Supermodel of the World.* I figured why not stake my claim and go the whole way? Eric Kupper was brought in to pro-

Just as long as you call me, baby.

duce and brought that classic disco in the nineties feel to it. When it was finished, I got my friend Felix Prince to record some links and segues in between the tracks.

I had always wanted Aunt Esther from *Sanford and Son* to be on my record, and so we called up her manager and started negotiations. Well, Lawanda may not be in the public eye anymore, but she likes to get paid—and how. I flew her in from her home in South Central Los Angeles. The day she came to the studio I was slightly tense because I wanted to get a quick in-the-studio press shot with her. But up until the moment she saw me, I had thought it best not to tell her that I was a drag queen. When we finally came face to face she did not bat an eyelid.

Because she was costing me such a fortune I thought that I would record everything she said from the moment she walked into the studio so I could be sure to get my money's worth. The very first thing she said when she got into the studio was, "Tell the man with the money to come here and pay me." I laughed and laughed and laughed, and that line became the opening line of and inspiration for a whole new song called "A Shade Shadey (Now Prance)."

The next thing was the photo shoot, and for that I called on the talents of photographer Mark Contratto. Now, before a fashion shoot the secret is to drink a cup of vinegar because it shrinks the stomach. I am also an avid advocate of my patented supermodel Tic Tac Diet: a Tic Tac for breakfast, a Tic Tac for lunch, and for dinner no Tic Tac—just a glass of water. Naturally, I don't live by any of these guidelines—and neither should you. Instead, do as I do, which is to eat like a pig and then put on a strapping corset to suck it all in.

We did the shoot at Industria—Supermodel Central—and Mathu and Zaldy did makeup and styling. They also created the orange body suit and the red ruffled skirt that was the supermodel outfit. We styled it after

ONLY
ONE PERSON
PER STALL

*Some of the best times I've had in a
nightclub have been in the ladies' room.*

Versace in the days before he was on the phone volunteering his services! It was designed quite scientifically to show my feminine parts, which are my legs and my oh-so-thin waist.

In that outfit I felt like a caped crusader, and that's what it's all about, transformation from being an ordinary person into a superhero. On my way to the shoot I had worn my daytime disguise, a Clark Kent preppy drag. It was my way of being invisible. I had no eyebrows, no hair, and in khakis and glasses the camouflage was complete, a way of blending into the background so that no one could even see me. I didn't need to wear the glasses, but they were just another screen, another layer. Whether you are Superman or Supermodel saving the world is high profile stuff. It can really take it out of you. So you need an ordinary persona so that you can catch a cab, go to the bank, and go about your business without a lot of unwelcome attention.

DRAG NAMES: MIX & MATCH

FIRST	LAST
Tasha	DuBois
Tanesha	Lamour
Tina	Deville
Chena	Keisha
Sheena	Antoinette
Stanika	Thomas
Skunketta	Black
Aneka	Zena
Erika	White
Yetiva	Butts
Sasha	Shepard
Diandra	Andrews
Lahoma	Scott
Tawny	Brown
Tandy	Seville
CoCo	Fox
Sable	Alexander
Tiffany	Fairchild
Melissa	Jones
Brittany	PotatoHead
Afrika	Rivers
Freida	Nevada
Misty	LaCroix
Samantha	ThunderPussy
Crystal	St. Laurent
Gayma	Monroe
Gina	St. Germain
Chocolate	Middlesex
Felicity	Savage
Octavia	Ariagus
Octopussy	Ross
Taylor	Douglas
Cherry	Cane
Candy	Foster
Missy	Jones
Nicole	Snow
Ashley	Shantay
Chantal	Galore
Charlie	Rose
Toni	Davis
DeeDee	King
Nikki	Love
Sheba	Adams
Apple	Crawford
Trina	Bliss
Whitney	Chanel
Amanda	Goodfellow
Selena	Houston
Vicki	Summers
Kelly	Jackson
Rene	Richards
Sweetie	VanZant
Shiquitta	Matthews
Sabrina	Joy
Peaches	Mayday
Bertha	Bloomingdale
Princess	McElroy
Vida	Johnson
Lizette	Green
Hagatha	Blue
Marrisa	Cruise
Shuga	Perry
Foxy	Day

Once I was in that outfit I felt like a supermodel all right. I was the queen bee. It was fierce, assertive, and royal. And it sent just the right kind of message the Supermodel of the World would want to send to keep any challenging bitches at bay! I love the final shot I chose for the cover. It's quite a good pose, because it isn't a pose, really. It doesn't look contrived—even though it is! Of course, it's all an illusion. The real scoop is I'm wearing just one pair of cheap Woolworth stockings.

Chapter 14

You Better Work

I performed Supermodel for the first time at Wigstock Labor Day of '92. There was a strong buzz about the single coming out, and the welcome I got both backstage and onstage was very different from the year before. The single was released on my birthday, November seventeenth. From that moment on I started doing dates. I launched the Supermodel world tour in Atlanta, and from there went on to every city in America. It lasted for well over a year— straight through January of '94 when I opened for Duran Duran in Hartford, Connecticut.

In the early days I went by myself, with just my costume and a DAT tape. The promoters would pick me up at the airport and they were always surprised that I was on my

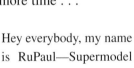

own, that I didn't have an entourage. It was fine back then, it was much more personal, and the promoters would take me round and show me things. But once the single started tak-ing off and the video started playing, I couldn't do that anymore. Especially when I got to Cleveland.

The show I did was pretty much the same all over. I would begin with Supermodel wearing a bathing suit ensemble that showcased my legs. Then I would go straight into "House of Love." After that I stopped the tape and did my monologue. And just in case you missed it, here it is one more time . . .

Wigstock '92.

Hey everybody, my name is RuPaul—Supermodel of the world! How do you like my outfit? This is the front [pause while I turn around] and this is the back [wild applause]. Oh, I bet you say that to all the queens [laughter]. I have traveled thousands of miles to be with you tonight, to bring you a message, probably the most important message you'll ever hear in your entire life. And the message is, Ladies and Gentlemen, *You Better Work.* [Uproar] No, actu-ally, the real message is this: Learn how to love yourself [quick pause] learn how to love yourself, 'cause if you don't love yourself, how in the hell are you gonna love somebody else. [uproar] Can I get an Amen in here? [Amen.] It's the truth, it's the truth, baby, I'm a living witness. If I'm lying I'm flying and you don't see no wings do you? [Pause] Well you might see some wings on Maxi Pad, but you don't see none on my back. [Laughter] The day I started loving myself was the day I became Supermodel of the World.

Supermodel *tour '93.*

Love can move mountains. Love is the answer. Everybody say love. [Love.] *Everybody* say love. [Love.] Now drive that down the [insert local reference here—The New Jersey Turnpike, the L.A. Freeway, the Thames River, the Autobahn, the Champs Elysées]. Now get your ass outta here.

You know what they say, "Big hair, big heart."

The second part of my monologue involved taking a few questions from the audience, and the truth is they ask me the same questions all the time. So whenever I am asked how tall I am—which is all the time—I say, "Honey, with hair, heels, and attitude I'm through the motherfuckin' roof." Or, "Tall enough to give you a Shaq Attack." Or "Taller than your mama."

Some things get better the more you say them. The audience never seems to tire of me saying in that Ed McMahon voice, "You better work, bitch." It's become a mantra. And I'll be saying "Everybody say love" till my dying day. These are not catch phrases with sell-by dates— these are eternal truths. "If you don't love yourself—how in the hell you gonna love somebody else?" That's another old favorite, and even if that was the only thing I ever said in my whole life, it would be worth it. It's certainly the truest. That and "Learn how to love yourself."

Anyway, after the question-and-answer session I retired from the stage for a quick costume change. I would slip into my Supermodel cape, a gorgeous white taffeta thing. It's my homage to Diana Ross. Then, when I went back on, I would do Supermodel, and at the end I would select a few supermodels from the audience to come up on stage and work the runway. It never took much to persuade them to come up on stage and take off their shirts, even their bras, and even, on one or two occasions, everything they had on. I would cheer on encouragment, making sure that every supermodel who walked across my stage got a big round of applause.

Normally, it all went fine. Something about a drag queen commands respect—people would only come up when invited, and only then one at a time. But by the time I got to Cleveland the Supermodel phenomena had reached boiling point. All of a sudden people started coming up one after another, and soon the whole audience was swamping the stage. So I just sweetly said "Goodnight everybody," and ran into my dressing room. It was out of the frying pan into the fire, because there I was drying off and catching my breath when this young transygirl burst in shivering and shaking. She was half sobbing, half screaming, so that the words could barely come out. I couldn't understand what she was saying, but she was jabbing a CD toward me, so I just grabbed it, signed it, and said, "Thanks, sweetie." It made me nervous because she was nervous, and I picked up on that. That type of hysteria is scary because it's really out of control, and from that moment on I knew that when I went out on the road, I needed someone with me.

Generally, with one or two exceptions, everything's

Working lower lashes.

always the same on the road—even the other queens working the disco circuit. When I was on the first leg of the Supermodel tour it was Martha Walsh, Marky Mark, and CeCe Penniston. I either just missed them, or they were leaving tomorrow, or coming next week. When I finally met Martha Walsh she said, "I feel like I know you—I was always on the week before you or the week after you."

Most of the time I had very good experiences, but every now and again you get the club owner from hell, like the time I was in Key West. I did my show, but when I got offstage the club owner announced that I was going to do an encore. I didn't have an encore to do,

1. Versace: I'm living for one of his crocodile mini trench coats
2. Valentino: If ever I were to go to the Oscars, I'd go in Valentino
3. Todd Oldham: An American classic. I ordered about twenty pairs from his new shoe collection
4. Bob Mackie: Cher! Cher! Cher!
5. Rifat Ozbek: Just about the only reason to go to London
6. Pamela Dennis: Timeless creations that I wear on special occasions (like in the *Little Drummer Boy* video)
7. Thierry Mugler: Fit for a drag queen
8. Karl Lagerfeld: Every girl should have a Chanel suit in her closet
9. Isaac Mizrahi: He understands women's bodies (and men-who-dress-like-women's bodies)
10. Christian Lacroix: Sweetie, Lacroix, sweetie
11. Claude Montana: Gorg!
12. Herve Legere: Form-fitting fabulousness

which, very politely, I told him. But he was drunk and on God knows what, so when he heard that he went off. "I carried your towel, I dried you off" he said, as he began listing all the things he had done for me. He became hysterical. In all my twelve years in clubs I have never seen anything like that before. I could not get out of there fast enough!

But the good times more than cancelled out the bad times. I had started the Supermodel tour in Atlanta, and six months later I went back there to really enjoy the phenomena of it all. Although I'd been home a couple of times over the past few years, this was the first time I felt like a homecoming queen. When I got to the airport I was expecting Dick Richards and the Peek sisters to pick me up in their station wagon. But, instead, there was a stretch limo waiting to take me to the Ritz Carlton. Things had really changed, although the station wagon would have been just fine.

The shows were packed, really packed. The crowd was so thick all around the stage there was no way to get back-stage to change my costume between numbers.

Bloomingdale's asked me to perform at an in-store promotion. They also had windows with RuPaul-inspired mannequins.

So I had to have security escort me out to the parking lot, where I took off my dress between two parked cars, and ran back inside. In spite of my reputation for being a Glamazon, the truth is I can change almost any-where in a pinch. Sure, every queen likes to have fancy schmancy dressing rooms with fresh-cut flowers, but in a pickle any old parking lot will do. Why, right outside Bloomingdale's and en route to a television inter-view at the Plaza, I hiked my dress up, untucked, undid my waist cincher, yanked the dress down—and that was that, right there on the street. It takes a bit of practice but in an emergency it can be done. Although the street was jammed with people, I swear my only witness was a Scottish terrier who looked like he'd just laid eyes on a big fat juicy T-bone steak—which of course he had! I've also changed in front of the New York Public Library on Fifth Avenue for a TV shoot. This was a complete costume change, so I had some members of the crew hold up a drape around me as a sort of portable dressing room.

One of the favorite things I liked to do on the Supermodel tour were in-store signings. When the record was first released I did one in New York at Sam Goody's. Then I did one in L.A. at the Virgin Mega Store on Sunset Boulevard. Each of these was a complete zoo, but the best one of all was the one I did in Atlanta at Turtles record store in Buckhead. The turnout was phenomenal. Everyone I ever knew was there—Floydd's entire family, the whole Funtone gang, teenagers who wanted me to sign their heads, and even mothers with their newborn babies. I was there for three hours and the crowd was still pouring in. In the end they had to close the doors—which I did feel bad about—and I left through the back door. On the way back to the hotel I had the limo take me through Midtown, my old neighborhood. It was just a bunch of burnt-out buildings—no more discos, barely anyone on the street. I stopped at Krispy Kremes donuts, went back to my hotel, pigged out, and then passed out.

Most of the time on the road you're in the airport in transit and you wake up in the morning and don't know what city you're in. To offset this Twilight Zone feeling, I have things I bring with me to create a home away from home.

The first and most important toy to have at one's disposal is a stretch limosine. Now I know what you're thinking: "That old queen likes a big old stretch so she can feel important." Exactly right! But the truth is with the hair, heels, and attitude I *am* through the roof. In the early days of the tour my manager tried to cart me to the gig in his Volkswagen Rabbit. We couldn't put the roof down because it was raining, and even with the front seat all the way down, it was quite a crush. As we pulled up outside the club there was a line all the way around the block, and they could all see me, laid out like something out of *Frankenstein*. *Not* a glamourous way to make an entrance. And that—apart from the leg room—is the other

I feel most at home when I'm in a hotel.

attraction of stretch limos: tinted windows. What is the use of getting all dolled up to make a spectacular entrance if you blow it by arriving in a VW for all to see?

I always take my stuffed donkey Jimmy with me. He's the ideal companion—old and loved. He has only one eye. I found him dumped on the street after Christmas in '86. There were bags stuffed with old toys just discarded. Someone must have gone through them because they were scattered all over the street. I saw him lying there in the gutter and said, "I've got to have him." He goes with me everywhere, and I guess he has seen everything.

On the road, and at home, I entertain myself just like a child. I've always loved pop culture, and I think that the tools of pop culture—the VCR, camcorder, and CD player—are like crayons in a child's playroom. I use these toys in the same way to color my world and keep myself entertained.

From the time I was twelve I would cut pictures out of

Some of the most unforgettable women in the world . . . are men.

Vogue magazine and paste the pictures of my favorite models on the wall. I still do that today, sticking up pictures from magazines on the walls of my hotel and dressing room.

Around the same age my father gave me a Panasonic cassette recorder, and I would make homemade comedy tapes like the famous ones, *Superfly Meets Shaft,* where they would say, "Superfly, I'm from the *National Examiner,* how do you feel about Superfly's wife?" and then, for a reply, they would play a snatch from "Me and Mrs. Jones." I would make my own cut-up tapes. Although I no longer make those tapes, I do make compilation tapes of my favorite artists. I have a Walkman and CD player with little, portable, battery-operated speakers, so I can hear music wherever I go. I always bring incense with me too—it goes with the music and adds to the atmosphere.

I also bring my compilation video tapes of Diana Ross, Cher, and others. Although there is always television in the limos, the reception can be lousy, so I just pop in one of my tapes. Contemplating my heroes in this way is also a good way for me to psych myself. It helps me visualize the superstar inside, and get me ready to prance around on stage.

Throughout the whole Supermodel tour I had my Hi-8 video camera with me, and, inspired by my friend Nelson's example, I taped everything and everyone. We used footage from my travels exclusively for the video for "A Shade Shadey (Now Prance)." I have also transferred my favorite movies to Hi-8. In case my room does not have a VCR, I can hook my camcorder up to the television and watch movies that way.

The only other thing about being on the road is this: When staying in hotels, always remember to bolt and chain the door. At any given moment hotel maids, staff, and personnel can burst into your room, unannounced, either to check the minibar, turn down your bed, or any number of things. I can't tell you how many times I have been shocked shitless by someone barreling in to service the room.

Shooting the videos for the singles proved to be a welcome break from the treadmill of life on the road. Perhaps "break" is the wrong word, because they were so exhausting! The concept for the *Supermodel* video was a simple narrative beginning with the little girl who lived in the Brewster projects of Detroit. She is discovered by an *Ebony* Fashion Fair talent scout and goes on to become the Supermodel of the World. Her life is a glamourous whirl of fashion shoots, although gradually it all becomes too much and she goes crazy, cavorting in the fountain and finally closing in on the camera, a dead ringer for Gloria Swanson doing her closeup in *Sunset Boulevard*. Sound familiar? Of course it does! Any similarity to *Mahogany* is totally deliberate.

We used Alphabet City on the Lower East Side for the Brewster projects, and the first thing we shot, as soon as it was light, was the little girl supermodel, because she had to be at school by 8:30 A.M. This gave me a little bit more time to get ready for my first take. In this scene my character returns for a triumphant fashion shoot to the very same spot where she was discovered as a little girl. The shoot begins as she steps out of the trailer. This scene was a big thrill for me, not only because I was wearing a sparkling Todd Oldham dress but also because it was the first time I had had my own Winnebago, which is the hallmark of any high-class location shoot. From there we went all over the city shooting exteriors, from the West Village to Central Park, from rooftops with the Empire State Building in the background to the sidewalk outside the Moondance diner. For that particular shot I was wearing a red gingham French waitress number. I was supposed to be cuddling a small dog. However, the props department came up with a dog that was almost bigger than me. Lifting that sucker nearly broke my back.

My favorite shot in the whole video was with the little girls who had just got out of school and were hanging out in their uniforms of gray pleated skirts and blue blazers. I said, "Hey, you guys want to be in a shot?" In unison they said "Yeah!" and we all joined hands and sashayed down the sidewalk right outside the Plaza. It's such a beautiful shot. You can see straight down Fifth Avenue for blocks and blocks and blocks with crowds of people all around. Epic. Later we found out that one of the

Supermodel *video montage.*

girls was the daughter of Naomi Sims, the world's first
black supermodel. But the real star of that group was the
little cocoa-brown girl with straight golden hair. I was
holding her hand, and she looked so happy, moving her
hips and shaking her hair like a real supermodel. She was
fabulous!

We shot the video in October—so it was a little chilly
for the infamous fountain scene in *Mahogany* where Diana
falls in and splashes round happy as a bird in a bath.
Instead of the Trevi in Rome that they used in the movie,
we had to make do with the fountain outside the Plaza.
Randy Barbato, my manager who was directing the video,
fully expected me to be arrested since we had not dared get
permission to film in the fountain. In the eventuality that I
was arrested, he had secretly planned to carry on filming,
and cut in the footage of me being led away shivering and
in handcuffs into a waiting police car. I think he was disappointed when I did not get arrested. It was very New
York, no one seemed to think anything of a drag queen
prancing round in a fountain at sunset. Mercifully, it was
the last shot of the day, because after I had been under that
fountain I was a shivering wreck, my makeup ruined
beyond repair.

We shot the video in two days—one day of exteriors
in black and white and one day in the studio in color. All in
all I had about eighteen costume changes and nine hair
changes. Mathu and Zaldy were my stylists and made
appearances in the video too.

When I saw the rough cut I got up out of the editing
suite and did that dance that football players do when they
make a touchdown, screaming and howling for about five
minutes. Finally, I had arrived. I was a star. I cried. Real
tears. The video became a staple in all the clubs, and went
on to win two *Billboard* video awards and a bunch of others. It was also nominated for best dance video on MTV
Music Video Awards.

The video for my second single, "Back to My Roots,"
was much more ambitious, even though I opted out of
doing any exteriors and went instead for two days of inte-

riors, thinking that this would be more practical. How wrong I was. This time we had twice as many costume changes, three times as many hair changes, a cast of thousands of extras, and a stretch limousine so long it only just fit into the studio. In short, all the elements of disaster. But the video was fierce.

The song was all about the black hair revolution. Black hair real-

Baby doll curls.

I dream of Jeannika.

ly is the most fabulous over the top thing that there is. Growing up, the myth was you couldn't do anything with black hair. WRONG. Today there are the most incredible hair sculptures, braids, and accessories. I sample some of them in the song—but I really only just scratch the surface.

Again the concept was a loose rags to riches narrative, and it was dedicated to my mother. The video began with Mama doing people's hair in the kitchen

Afro puffs.

Jheri curls.

and went on to show my brilliant career as a hairdresser with my own home shopping show. At the end I went back to my roots in Atlanta, to my Mama's own hair salon. Lawanda Page played my mother, and because my real mother was such a big fan of hers, I could not wait for her to see the finished thing. To top it off, I gave Lawanda a big hug at the end of the video,

The Back to My Roots *video featured classic Afro-American hair do's and don'ts. Here I am serving an assymmetrical shroom.*

From left to right: Lawanda Page, me, and cast members from the Back to My Roots *video.*

and the words "I love you, Mama" were written across the screen. Even though she would have just said, "Aw, nigger, you *are* crazy!" I knew Mama would love it.

Because we had been shooting, I hadn't slept in three days. Before any big day I never sleep the night before—I am simply too excited. I perform best on overdrive, running on empty. But once it was done there was no time to refuel! It was straight off to the big march on Washington where over a million lesbians and gays were marching on the White House to make their presence known to the new administration and the people of America. On Friday night we flew to Baltimore and performed at the Hippodrome for thousands of queens; the next night I performed at the Post Office in Washington, D.C., for thousands more; and then on Sunday at the rally for what seemed like the entire gay population of the planet.

I woke up that morning feeling refreshed in an antique bed at the Jefferson, a hotel not half a block away from the White House. The first thing I put on—even before ordering breakfast—was Martha Wash's "Carry On," which for me is one of the truly great anthems of self-love and perseverance:

> Still can hear the way
> Mama used to say
> Never
> Never let your spirit bend
> Never
> Never give in to the end
>
> I CARRY ON

When I heard it I just started crying. And for some reason I could not stop playing the tape over and over. I was standing there in my hotel room, holding my hands up in the air and saying, "Yes, yes," with tears pouring down my cheeks. While I got ready I continued to listen to it— there just didn't seem anything else to play that day.

I arrived at the march wearing a black tube dress and Birkenstocks. Thank God for sensible shoes, because we arrived in this big field with no one around to tell us where to go. So we had to hike across this field toward this big backstage tent. I found refuge in a trailer full of the world's most powerful dykes: Martina Navratilova, Melissa Etheridge, Lea Delaria, and practically every other lesbian celebrity in the western world. I was safe, but sweltering. I snuck into the back and changed into my Wonder Woman American flag outfit from the *Back to My Roots* video. It's incredibly snug-fitting, rather like wearing contact wallpaper. Now, when it's hot most women glow. I, however, sweat like an absolute pig. It was a miracle my entire face didn't fall off in a makeup landslide. Practically melting, I decided to wait outside in the open air by the side of the stage until it was my turn to go on.

So there I was, waiting by the staircase to the podium, when I saw Jesse Jackson walking in my direction. I was sure he was looking at someone behind me, but when I looked around there was no one there. He was heading my way and closing fast! Oh my God! "Oh no, you're not going to get away from me!" he said, shaking my hand, and introducing me to the rest of his entourage. Before we could really get acquainted they announced my name. As I made my way up the ramp Cybill Shepherd was just coming off stage. She screamed when she saw me and said, "You look incredible." As I went out on stage and looked out, all I could see was this cloud of dust as people rushed to the front of the stage. I launched into the beginning of "Supermodel" and noticed someone on the side of the stage waving their arms frantically. I thought they were trying to get my attention, but it turns out that they were doing sign language. When the song was done, I said a few choice words: "People always ask me where I'll be in ten years, and I say 'In ten years I'll be in the White House.' Miss Thing goes to Washington! Paint the mother pink!" I left out "fucker" because we were on television worldwide.

About an hour later, still riding high on the experience of performing, I got a call with the news that my mother had passed away in the night, and that's when it all came together—playing that Martha Wash track over and over, and crying like a baby. Mama was saying goodbye and telling me that everything was going to be all right and that I should carry on.

In a way I was glad because she had been sick for a long time. The last time I had seen my mother was in February. At that point she could not hear in one ear, and she couldn't walk, so they put her bed in the living room so that she could be at the center of things. We watched the piece MTV News did on me at the mall in New Jersey together. Introducing the piece, Kurt Loder made some

The outfit I wore to the March on Washington.

lame he/she pun, and me and my mother looked at each other laughing. I think she finally understood the whole thing, and she was so proud. Not that she would ever admit that if she were here today. She went to her grave as Leo the lion, fierce and ruling. Even at her funeral, people got up and said, "You know, Toni was the kind of person you either liked or you didn't." I couldn't help laughing when I heard that.

As long as I live I will not forget standing on that stage and looking out over a sea of people—it looked like millions—toward the Washington Monument. The clouds were piled up on either side, and in the distance a plane was coming in to land at National Airport. It was a heavenly moment, standing there on that stage on the same spot where Martin Luther King had once stood before me.

I really feel that on that very special day, my mom and I both found freedom.

15 Chapter
Transy-Europe Express

Having succesfully toured America, the challenge for me now was to conquer Europe. The first stop was the Cannes Film Festival. I was there to perform at a very chichi benefit for Cinema Against AIDS. The dinner was to be held at a fancy restaurant in the Camargue, high in the hills above Cannes. My appearance went smoothly, but was nothing compared to my rendezvous with Elizabeth Taylor. Meeting her was like being ushered into the presence of God herself. I think I said something stunning and dazzling like, "Hello, how are you?" She seemed to know who I was. We were both standing on the photographer's seamless backdrop being arranged and positioned for our photograph to be taken, when she said, "I think I'd better

get you a chair, otherwise I'll be dwarfed by you."
I nearly collapsed. She was going to stand and I
was going to sit? In the presence of the goddess herself? It
was inconceivable. Anyway, someone else got the chair, I
sat down, and said, "Do you think I should cross my legs or
keep them like this?"

She said, "I think they look better just like that."

And that's why I did not cross my legs.

We took about eight pictures, and Liz stood there radi-
ating her stately supernova glamour. Then we shook hands
and she was escorted out. As she left the restaurant everybody fell silent, watching the queen leave. She glided past
the tables and then was gone.

For the "Back to My Roots" maxi single, I did a bonus
track called "Strudelmodel," a joke version in which the
young girl grows up in Hamburg instead of the Brewster
Projects. It has a life-is-a-cabaret-style piano arrangement
and I say, "You better vork" instead of "You better work."
Never in my wildest dreams did I think I'd actually end up
in Hamburg. But I did. And I will never forget it.

I had just come off a week of promotion hell in
England. It had rained all week, and the record company
had had me on a treadmill. Child, I barely had enough time
to take off my face before I had to put it back on again. I
swear you could see black rings under my eyes through my
foundation. It was from this experience that the concept of
monkey time comes. Monkey time is when you've been up
for days doing interviews doing shows and it all rolls into
one. Monkey time happens when you have to get up at 3:00
A.M. to do a 6:00 A.M. appearance on Breakfast TV, and
then you have press interviews all morning—one every
twenty minutes—same questions, same photos, and then
you have to go off for soundcheck, and then you do not one
show but two shows, with TV interviews both before and
after the show. Oh yes, it's all supposed to be in a day's
work, and I know you mustn't grumble, but there comes a
point when you finally lose your marbles. There comes a
point when you have been going "Blah blah blah" all day,
and suddenly the words won't come out right anymore and

Me and Elizabeth Taylor.

all you can do is go "Blah blah blah" for real. In fact that
was word for word the answer I gave when I was asked in
one interview what my feelings were about something or
other. That's monkey time. Your energy turns inside out
and everything's funny because you're so giddy. As I prat-
tled my "Blah blah blah" answer I remember the interviewer looked truly stunned. As he fumbled for his next
question, I screamed, "Please, please—does anyone have a
gun? Shoot me!" I was only trying to make him feel better,
but I think I just scared him all the more. The interview
ended shortly after that. But it was only midnight, and this
old horse had two more shows to go!

I made it through the week. Somehow. But things only
got worse. After finally leaving England and making it to
Hamburg, I found myself putting on my face in a weird
hotel room where the doors opened the wrong way, and
eating sausage sandwiches for lunch. The phone rang. It
was management calling with an update. They went on

about photo shoots and my next music video, but I could tell there was something else. My album had finally just come out that week and I was waiting to hear what number it was on the chart. To tell you the truth, it'd seemed like so long since I'd touched American soil, I had stopped thinking about it.

"I can't believe I forgot," I finally said, "did you get the chart numbers?" There was a pause on the other end.

And then they told me.

My album had debuted on the hot 100 at 109.

109.

Never in my worst nightmares did I think that it would debut below 50. I was shocked and amazed!

This was a sad Supermodel moment.

One oh nine.

One hundred and nine.

No, it didn't matter how you said it, it was still dire.

All I could do was keep chanting to myself, "109, 109, 109 . . ."

I was losing my M. I. N. D.

I am a pro, but this time I thought, the show will *not* go on. I tell you I was at my wit's end. My entire dressing ritual was disrupted. Not to mention the fact the record company people were sticklers for detail, and were not very understanding of the fact that Miss Charles was running behind schedule. They were pacing the halls, banging on the door, and did everything but call in Herr Fire Marshal to get me out of my room.

Finally, I got myself together, got into their tiny BMW, and made it to the television studio where I was to do a press conference and a television appearance. They kept reminding me that this was not just any television appearance, that it was the German version of the *Tonight Show*. I wasn't really listening to them. That terrible number 109 was still looping in my head as though I were having some kind of nightmare. Then they told me that one of the guests would be Karl Lagerfeld of the house of Chanel. After I had performed I was to join him on the panel of guests for conversation or "couch time," as they call it in

the biz. This might turn out okay after all, I thought.

But first there was the press conference. It was surreal! There were maybe twenty journalists sitting round a circular table—very Dr. Strangelove. But not one of them asked a single question. I find that this happens quite often in foreign parts—the press just doesn't know what to ask. Not even the simplest, tiniest question, like, oh, I don't know, Are you having a nice day? In these situations there is only one thing to do: go on autopilot and ask the questions yourself: "You probably want to ask me if I am having a nice day, and I am having a lovely day because blah blah blah." Sometimes I start speaking in tongues out of sheer frustration, although they seem to enjoy that just as much.

From that scintillating experience it was off to the television studio for the taping. They had this giant hemispherical world that I was to stand in. It would turn and I would be revealed. But the mechanism was faulty, so it would stop-start, stop-start, and I had to hold onto the thing

Some advice: Never wear high heels in soggy grass, and never perm your own hair.

RuPAUL'S FAVORITE CARS

1. 1966 Oldsmobile Toronado
2. 1969 Cadillac Eldorado
3. 1973 Buick Riviera
4. 1972 Mercedes Benz 280SL
5. 1994 Mercedes 500SL
6. 1968 Ferrari Daytona
7. 1994 Jeep Grand Cherokee 4 x 4
8. 1994 Ford Mustang Convertible
9. 1976 Corvette Stingray
10. 1970 Ford El Camino

for dear life, otherwise I would be spun out onto the studio floor a dizzy mess.

But that was just the tip of the iceberg. Because the television studio was union-organized—it was the most ancient studio on the planet and obviously had not been touched since the end of the Second World War—we had to be there three hours before the show started. And that was not all. Of course we had to do a rehearsal, but we had to do it in complete drag because they filmed it! Yikes! Moreover, they had all these lines taped on the studio floor, and I was given precise instructions NOT to go over them. So much as one toe out of place and I thought they would shoot me.

And it got worse. I had left my hair in the car. For a minute I thought about going bald, and featuring a Fraulein from hell look. But I always, always carry some extra hair in my bag, for just such an emergency. However, this ratty old wig needed work and the German hairdresser, bless his gay heart, was completely crazy and spoke no English. I kept on waving my hands in the air and saying "Higher! higher!" but he just did not understand. In the end we made it work. Somehow.

Every cloud has a silver lining, and in this case it was that fact I was going to be interviewed and meet the great Karl Lagerfeld, muse of Supermodels all over the world. If it weren't for that I would have told them all that I loved them very much, but they could take the sauerkraut and stuff it. You can imagine my reaction when two minutes before I was due to go on they said, "We're really sorry, but we have too many guests. We won't have time to interview you."

Something inside of me snapped. 109 and then this. I knew what I was going to do. Funny enough, I did one of the best performances of "House of Love" I've ever done.

The producers were thrilled. Then I did "Supermodel." I started out okay, never crossing the chalk lines the producers had drawn, but during the model rap part, I knew my time had come. I walked beyond the lines, forcing the camera crews, mouths gaping, to follow me. As I made my dash for freedom, I could see all the stagehands going mad in the shadows, waving their arms, frantically gesturing for me to go back. No way! I walked into the middle of the studio and right over to the table around which the panel, including Mr. Lagerfeld, was sitting. And I didn't stop there. I climbed right up on that table and lay right across it, serenading Karl. He looked genuinely surprised and delighted. Swiveling round I blew him a kissy-face and returned to my spot where I completed the song.

All was in an uproar when I got off stage, everyone going on about what I did on live television. I was ready to go home. But I was so exhilarated we took the car from the studio and went—in full drag—to the McDonald's in Frankfurt, where I got two quarter-pounders with cheese. Then I went back to my hotel and slept for twenty-four hours.

Chapter 16

Hollywood Ho

After Europe I set my sights on Hollywood. I was living for some couch time on national TV and finally the *Arsenio Hall Show* offered it, and this was to be a major turning point. In the meantime momentum had been building. Suddenly people in Peoria were talking about this seven-foot black blond drag queen who came from nowhere. Little did they know that it had been a lifetime's work, because as far as the outside world was concerned it was just the last few months of hype and promotion. I didn't mind, though. I just loved the idea of someone's mom making their kid a peanut butter and jelly sandwich for lunch and the kid yelling out, "You better work, Mom!"

The day of the taping we arrived at Paramount studios

at midday. I had not slept a wink the night before. I was scheduled to do a rehearsal with the band and then there was the three-hour transformation process. The record label people were pretty nervous about me performing with a live band and all, but frankly I was more anxious about the couch time.

The entire staff at Arsenio was as sweet as could be and very accommodating. Soundcheck went fine, which I did working a preppy realness look: denim shirt, khaki pants, shaved head and, of course, five-inch pumps from Fredericks of Hollywood. I also practiced in my gorgeous white tulle supermodel cape. As usual I planned to walk out, twirl it around a few times, and then toss it, à la Miss Ross.

We went back up to the dressing room and began on my face. Mathu came from New York to do my makeup and help with my Zaldy creation. He knew how nervous I was, so he just let me be as he painted away. Before long, it was time to go on. I was escorted from the makeup room to the backstage area. I looked great, I felt great, I was ready. Everyone who works on the show was hanging out at the backstage area ooohing and aaahing over me. It was kind of comforting. I just smiled and kept focusing on what I was gonna say, what I was gonna do. I was a nervous wreck, but I didn't let a soul know.

Finally, I was called on stage and Arsenio introduced me. I performed "Supermodel," and the only thing I really remember from the performance was the twirl at the beginning. The rest was really all a blur—except the applause at the end!

Thank God for commercial breaks. I had a few minutes to touch up my makeup, adjust my fierce ruling tuck, and then position myself on the couch for the chat. I don't remember much about this either, it seemed to happen so quickly. Arsenio instantly made me feel at ease, and he also gave me the room to do my thing. It's hard to describe what's going on in one's head at a moment like that. You know there are about five million things you want to say. Hundreds of jokes and gags you've saved for this very

Me and my managers. From left to right: Randy Barbato, me, and Fenton Bailey.

moment, and suddenly the lights are shining, the audience is watching, the clock is ticking, and you're babbling away like you've never babbled before. And then, before you know it, it's over.

Still, I do remember one or two morsels. One was the line "I'm just a regular Joe [beat] with the unique ability to accessorize." The other was Arsenio getting the signal from the floor manager to go to a commercial break—but he was having too much fun. In the end even I could see the guy motioning Arsenio to wrap it up. "One more minute, just get me one more minute," Arsenio said. I was elated, because there's no greater flattery in this world than to be able to hold up a commercial break—it feels like walking on air.

It could not have gone any better. People got to understand my platform, which is about loving yourself, understanding who you are, and bringing your uniqueness to the party. He loved me enough to ask me back twice more that same year. And I got an Arsenio bathrobe in black terrycloth with the show's logo embroidered on it!

But it wasn't over yet. CNN had a camera crew on the lot and wanted to do an interview. I did a quick costume change and we went down to a waiting golf cart to take me to another part of the Paramount lot for the interview. Now you can imagine me trying to fit my big, tall ass in a golf cart. The hair alone was too big for that sucker. I had to be positioned horizontally to fit into the golf cart, with one end of me sticking out one side and my legs hanging out the other end. Very glamourous. The interview was a breeze. I was so full of energy I think the

Me and Bill Cosby right before we taped The Arsenio Hall Show.

interviewer didn't really get a single question in. By the time that was done I ran off to the nearest bathroom and took off the dress, hair, corset, heels. What a relief! I slipped into my new Arsenio dressing gown and into the limo that was waiting outside.

We still weren't done. It was off to another photo shoot. This was for the L.A. Eyeworks advertising campaign. Driving to photographer Greg Gorman's studio, we noticed that we were being trailed. At first we thought we

Hollywood Ho

were imagining it, so we asked the driver to step on it and make some tricky turns. Sure enough, the car behind us followed. Eventually we stopped and my manager got out and confronted the people behind us. It turned out to be a car full of fans, and the driver was a drag queen. Can you imagine? In full do. It was such a sight. I got out of the car and we all took pictures. They were very sweet. They even presented me with a gift of golden high heels. To this day I still hear from the driver of that car.

Arsenio opened the floodgates, and after that I was invited on a number of television shows, becoming Miss Television. But no amount of appearances could prepare me for my date with Mr. Television . . .

Chapter 17

Mr. and Miss Television

It was a funky, hot day. Baking. The kind you only get in L.A. I was putting the finishing touches to my do in the air-conditioned cool of the Universal Sheraton hotel. I was wearing a Pamela Dennis gown in ink black, bejeweled with a thousand diamantes. It was the night of a thousand stars—and I was wearing them all! It had been almost a year of going all over the States and all around the world flogging "Supermodel," and after all that hard work this, I hoped, would be a day to savor.

Supermodel, the video, had been nominated as best dance video, and I was greedy to hold one of those little silver moonwalker statuettes in my hand. I had no idea what I would say by way of an acceptance speech, but I knew that once I was holding one of those mothers I would rise to the occasion. Whether I won or lost, I thought that either way the day would be a winner, because I was also going to present an award for favorite rock thing, which Aerosmith ended up winning.

Well, the Universe certainly has ways of suprising us.

Two days before the awards, I was told that my co-presenter was to be Milton Berle. Dear old Uncle Miltie. A lot of the MTV kids are simply too young to have any idea who he is—but I know because I have my TV education. He was famous for dressing up in drag and making fun of women with a kind of jackass Borscht Belt schtick. His brand of humor is not my brand of humor, so I was not too thrilled about this. The brilliant minds at MTV thought that it would be a great idea: old drag queen, new drag queen, stick them together and present an award! Sounds good. On paper.

The next day the script arrived—the script that Milton had written, and it was very unfunny. Very old TV. Not my thing at all. It made me realize that MTV didn't get what I was doing at all. They didn't get that my take on drag is all about love, saying that we are *all* drag queens. It's certainly not about putting women down. And it's not about being the butt of a bunch of cheap dick jokes.

Still, I thought I could handle it.

Gliding through the hotel lobby, I gave a cheery wave to Green Jelly, who were waiting for their ride, and I slipped into the limo feeling as cool, as crisp, and as full of expectation as an afterdinner mint.

From the outset it was just going to be one of those roller-coaster days. MTV had hired every limousine driver in the city. Everywhere you looked there was a stretch limo. We must have drawn the short straw, because even though the Universal amphitheater was just a short drive away from the Universal hotel on the Universal lot, our driver got lost. We must have gone past the *Jaws* exhibit about half a dozen times before we finally were dumped on the tarmac a couple of hundred yards away from the entrance. Having run the press gauntlet, it was the hike of a lifetime up and down stairs and along corridors as we were taken to where Milton Berle was waiting to rehearse his material.

When we arrived at his dressing room he had just finished eating a cheese cracker and was covered with crumbs. His wife was there too, applying mascara in the mirror, and a writer from MTV was also in the room. Uncle Miltie was having makeup applied from his waist up, and he had on a pair of boxer shorts. His pants were around his ankles. Immediately upon being introduced, he grabbed my fake breasts and honked them saying, "Hiya toots." Then he ordered everyone out of the dressing room, including his wife—who left—and my manager, who declined to leave. Since he was a television veteran, and since I respect elderly people, I was determined to be cordial and try to laugh at his jokes. But I had not expected this. Obviously, he was just thinking, "Oh, drag queen, Ha! Ha! Ha!" and as we rehearsed it became clear that he was just using me as a prop, as a piece of business. He had all the "funny" lines, and I was just there for him to wipe the floor with. He was a complete control freak about it too: "When you say this, say it like this . . . No! do it again, like this . . ." Even though I was in full makeup, he grabbed my face with his hand and moved my head around like I was some kind of mannequin or ventriloquist's dummy. I tell you, my blood was boiling, but I thought, "Okay, I'll go through this rehearsal, but when the time comes I'll do my own thing." It had worked in Germany.

Meanwhile, he had his hands all over me—honking my foam rubber breasts, grabbing my crotch, putting his hands all over my bottom—and I was pushing them off, thinking, "What is this?" If I had been Cindy Crawford, there would have been lawsuits flying all over the place within five minutes, and the show would *not* have gone on. He was also trying to pull up his pants the whole time, but for some reason they kept on falling down. The grossness of the whole situation really upset me.

As soon as it was over and as soon as I was out of the dressing room, I got mad at myself for letting him do that to me. All the time I kept thinking he's an old man, he's a show business legend, and I should show him respect even though he was showing me the greatest disrespect. I grew up with this mentality that you mustn't grumble and must keep a stiff upper lip. Yet why is it that because I'm a drag queen I'm supposed to take all that shit in my stride?

The next thing I knew I was rushed to my seat because they were about to start the show. I was still shaken up by what had just happened. I'm not a kitten, I've seen it all, but this really did shock me. Anyway, the show started, and I just hoped that I had an award to look forward to. When my category, best dance video, came up everyone in the audience screamed. But although I got the audience's vote, I didn't win. En Vogue won, with "Free Your Mind." I love them and I love that video—and that's all I am going to say. But by now I was stewing, and the thunder clouds gathered as it got nearer to having to do this thing with Milton Berle.

So they came and got me, brought me backstage, and said, "You're going to have to help hold him up and get him onstage." Now I have always helped little old ladies across the street, but I thought, "Oh brother, that's great. I can't walk out and make my entrance, because I am going to have to nursemaid Milton Berle who's just going to insult and abuse me." But stiff upper lip, mustn't grumble. Backstage while we were waiting to go on, they got a stool for him to sit on and after what seemed like an eternity, we were announced and out we went.

By this point I was really miffed, I'm seething and thinking, "This little fucker." The first thing he did, as I recall, was put his arm and shoulder across my tits as though he was leaning on them. That got him a cheap laugh. Then after some inane banter he threw me the line, "You know, RuPaul, thirty years ago when I was on television, I used to wear dresses." To which I was supposed to say, "How interesting. Why did you give it up?" This was all to set up his reply, which has to be one of the lamest jokes this side of the First World War: "Because it was a drag."

But of course, dear reader, you may know that I didn't say that. Instead when he said, "You know, RuPaul, thirty years ago when I was on television, I used to wear dresses," I simply said, "That's interesting. You used to wear dresses, and now you wear diapers." The line came to me out of the blue, and as I said it I thought, well, this is fair enough, this is part of that Borscht Belt humor. It was straight out of the book *The Milton Berle School of How to Be a Jackass,* ba-dum-ba-dum. I was just giving him the same that he was giving me—except it was a little bit funnier. Two people can make jokes at one another's expense. But then I remember the hush that fell over the audience. I could hear some people laugh and some people go "Oooh." It was almost like an earthquake had struck. It was this extraordinary thing. As a drag queen I was assigned this role of being the kitchen mop. But because I didn't play the role I was supposed to play, everyone got all huffy. Oh, sure, wipe the floor with a drag queen, but with an old man? How could you!

Then Aerosmith came out and we presented them with the award, and they threw me some shade. "See you, toots," Steven Tyler said. Christian Slater set the seal on the whole thing by coming back after the commercial break and saying what a nice guy Milton Berle was. And I suppose I was the Wicked Witch of the East. Well, for the record, he is not a nice guy, as many of the people who have worked with him have since told me. They are of the opinion he got just what he deserved that day. Of course, what I should have done in the dressing room is said, "Listen, motherfucker, get your goddamn hands off me," and then gone out there and been Miss Black America. I wish I had done that. But I didn't, and in spite of my regrets I did get to send the message that Miss Thing is not going to be treated like a doormat. Something, I have learned, that can work both for and against you.

The MTV Awards was my first surreal Hollywood experience—like something out of a Jackie Collins novel. There's no doubt that I did provide the drop-dead-oh-my-God-I-can't-believe-he-said-that moment of an otherwise boring show. The next day it was all over the papers, and I, the Queen of Everybody Say Love, was christened Rude Paul. And that was the worst part of it, because I have worked so hard not to be perceived as a bitchy queen who would read an old man, tearing him down to my level, which is what he was doing with me.

The very next day I flew back to New York. I dropped my bags and ran straight out of my apartment, out of drag, to go and get something to eat. There was this guy parked in his

> ## RuPAUL'S FAVORITE ACTORS
>
> It was hard for me to choose my favorite actors because so many of them are working that hyper macho thing, and to tell you the truth, the masculine aspect of our culture just doesn't appeal to me. Here are some exceptions.
> 1. Willem Dafoe: Menacing in *Wild at Heart*.
> 2. Charles Nelson Reilly: Work!
> 3. Paul Lynde: Funny as hell.
> 4. Matthew Modine: A sweet, sensitive man.
> 5. Brad Pitt: Something for everyone.
> 6. Richard Burton: A voice of gold.
> 7. Marlon Brando: An American classic.
> 8. Rip Taylor: Nobody does it better.

car talking to this guy on a bicycle. They didn't know me and I didn't know them, but they were reliving the whole thing. For a while Miltiegate was the story that would not lay down and die. I certainly provided him with a bit of free publicity. He dined out on that story with everyone from *Vanity Fair* to Howard Stern. For someone who supposedly rues the day he ever met me, he can't talk about it enough.

But, actually, to put it in perspective, there was something else that happened that day that was far more interesting than all that: I got to meet Courtney Love and Kurt Cobain. I was on my way back from the press tent having given them all a piece of my mind, and suddenly I heard these voices calling out, "Oh my God, look it's RuPaul!" I turned round and there they were—the King and Queen of America. They were like excited fans: "Oh my God I've got to get my picture taken with RuPaul!" said Kurt. As we were posing, Kurt explained how they had come to see me in Seattle, but by the time they got there my show was over and I was gone. Then Courtney handed me their baby,

Frances Bean. I think the baby's leg got scratched by one of my rhinestones because she started crying—either that or she needed her diaper changed.

They stick out in my mind from the nightmare zoo of that day. They were such nice, ordinary people. They weren't just schmoozing me—they were as thrilled to meet me as I was to meet them. It was a warm, wonderful, and genuine encounter.

I saw them again later in the year when I was on *Saturday Night Live,* and they, purely by chance, were the musical guests. Courtney and I ate lunch together in the canteen. It was the season premiere, and it was just like back-to-school day with the new kids on the block in one corner, not quite sure of the lay of the land, and the old pros in the other. Mike Myers didn't look too happy to be back at school. Anyway, Courtney and I gassed up a storm, and when the show was taping they came and took refuge in my dressing room from all the record company executives, business people, and hangers-on who were crowding out their dressing room. They even sang a bit of "We Wish You a Merry Christmas" for my television Christmas special (which was going to air that year on Channel Four in England). They really were so sweet, down to earth, and vulnerable.

And now, of course, Kurt is dead. He was young and beautiful and to the outside world had it all. After all, he was rich and successful and had made a real go of it doing what he loved to do, working with his creativity. But I think there's no getting around that twenty-something roadblock. That point in your life—astrologically when Saturn returns to your birthplace—when have to take a massive reality check. You finally have to face the fact that things are never going to be the way you thought they would be. It's at this point that you have to abandon many of the romantic ideas you had growing up—and that's hard because, until now, you've staked your life on them. Now, of course, this isn't an insurmountable problem; in fact it's a great opportunity for a richer and more challenging vision of life. But imagine if you had success at a young age, and

you're a star, and everyone's telling you that you're wonderful, fantastic. There's just one catch: You don't feel like
a star, and you don't feel wonderful or fantastic—in fact
you don't even feel like a human being. Each morning you
wake up feeling like shit and thinking, "Is this all there is?"

From left to right: Dave Grohl, me, Kurt Cobain, Courtney Love, Frances
Bean, and Krist Noveselic at the MTV Music Video Awards.

because all the glamour and the applause doesn't feel like
you thought it would. In fact, it doesn't feel like anything
at all. And if everyone's telling you how good you've got
it, how successful you are, how much you have achieved,
well, that must leave a pretty bitter taste in your mouth.

At least if you're down and out and feeling suicidal at
twenty-eight, you can steel yourself with the hope that
things will get better. But if you're twenty-eight and at the
top, you must not only feel pretty disappointed but also
trapped—for the only way for you to go is down. At least
that's my analysis. Sadly, it won't bring him back, and I
think we all wish that he had not gone.

My exchange with Milton Berle and encounter with
Kurt Cobain have both reinforced my belief about how
important it is to live your life according to no one else's
rules but your own.

There are so many rules imposed on us about what we should do, what we should say. Boys should be boys, and girls should be girls. But says who? Little boys should wear blue and little girls pink, you should not wear white shoes after Labor Day, you should not pick your nose. Tell me who says that? Where do these rules come from in the first place? Who says you can't bend over backwards and eat bugs if you want to? I guess the bugs would probably say you can't do that, but assuming that they are willing and consenting bugs, then there's no problem. Let's wig out eating bugs.

Seriously, these rules aren't our Creator's rules. If he had not wanted us to pick our noses, he would not have made it so that our fingers could fit in our noses, and, talking of orifices, he would have figured things out differently if he had not intended for boys to have sex with boys and girls to have sex with girls—in addition, of course, to boys and girls having sex with one another.

And it goes on from there: Men can't do this, women must do that, blacks mustn't do this, and gays can't do that. Okay, says who? I don't care if the President of the United States made a law about it tomorrow, if it's not true for you, forget about it. There is no higher authority on the planet, when it comes to deciding what's best for you, than you. Life is a banquet, so you should eat until you're full, and do as you please as long as you're not hurting anybody else.

So when people try and rein me in with rules and dos and don'ts, I have always thought that it is absurd, and on the many times that I have come up against this resistance, this tsk tsk tsk, I have always chosen to follow my heart rather than follow their rules.

You can't get satisfaction living your life according to someone else's rules. The second time I went on the *Arsenio Hall Show,* Bill Cosby was also a guest. Now, he had an ax to grind on that show, mainly about HBO's *Def Comedy Jam* which, in his opinion, showed black people degrading themselves with all the cussing and swearing. He said that it all went to show how black people were still enslaving themselves by getting themselves up as minstrels for the white man. Meanwhile there I was, this big black drag queen, waiting backstage for my turn. Not only was I wearing a huge white afro wig, but I was also wearing an outfit that I had had specially made; a watermelon outfit, in pink and green sequins.

But you know what? So what! Bill is perfectly entitled to have his opinion and speak his mind, and so am I. If I want to dress up in drag in a watermelon outfit, I will be the judge of whether I am playing the fool for the white man. And I can assure you that is *not* what I am doing.

That experience taught me that it's foolish to give what other people think about us so much credence. All that matters is how you feel about yourself. Do you love yourself? Ask yourself that question, right now, out loud and let the answer be *yes*. Some days you don't feel like getting out of bed and feel worthless. But don't ever ever give in to the tempation of not loving yourself. There is no reason—no matter what other people may think or say about you—not to love yourself. Because what other people may have to say about you is simply their opinion. It's not who you are. Their opinion about you is not reality. Reality is what is inside of you. So don't go falling for anybody else's crap. You can't control what others have to say about you. So don't worry about it. Save your energy for loving yourself, lighting yourself up like a lighthouse. And when the sun shines from inside it will create a beautiful glow that everyone will warm to.

Who made the rules? Who says black people have to be black? What is black? Is it the color of your skin? Do my freckles and light golden brown skin tone make me black or white? When Michael Jackson wrote the song "Black or White" he was saying it does not matter if you're black or white. Be whatever you want to be—that is the challenge—and feel free to use whatever you want to reinvent yourself as whatever you want.

This idea was always the inspiration for "Back to My Roots," because black hair is such a riot of creativity, an infinite number of choices and permutations. It can be every color, every style, and every shape. It's just like life, which can be whatever you want to be. All you have to do is live it out. And in the midst of the explosion of creativity you don't hear people complaining that one fabulous updo is trying to be white, trying to hide its blackness. They let hair be hair.

In the case of my own hair, if I put on a green wig, paint my face peanut butter and jelly stripes, and round it all off with a pair of antennae on my head (as I have) I would not expect to be told that I was trying to deny my blackness in order to become a Martian.

When I put on a blond wig, I am not selling out my blackness. Wearing a blond wig is not going to make me white. I'm not going to pass as white, and I am not trying to. The truth about the blond wig is so simple: It really pops. I want to create an outrageous sensation, and blond hair against brown skin is a gorgeous, outrageous combination.

I once said that I transcended the gay community, and some people have asked me just what I meant by that. What I meant is that yes, I am black, I am gay, and I am a man, and I love being all these things. But I cannot be defined by these things. There are millions of black gay men out there, but it would be disservice to sum any of them up in that way, because, while they may be those three things, they are so much more than that. My race, gender, and sexuality are a part of me, but that ain't the whole enchilada.

And while it is important to celebrate our differences in terms of race, sex, and gender, the thing that it is important to remember is that we all belong to one race—the human race. The fact is that we all really have more in common with each other than we think.

I think the problem is that sometimes we take things too seriously and get stuck on the details. The question is not who you are, but what do you bring to the party. What can you contribute, create, invent?

And that is why I never have and never will define myself based on my race, sex, or gender, all of which I love. I define myself as RuPaul.

RuPaul is an extension of the power that created this

universe, and we are all manifestations of its love. Therefore RuPaul can do everything, RuPaul is a boundless energy that can pour itself into whatever shape it wants. The wigs, the shoes, the corsets, the gowns, and the sequins are all gorgeous toys and I have come to this planet earth to play with them. And I am free to play with all the toys, and try on every damn outfit in the place if that's what I feel like doing.

Remember: This flesh, this body, is just a temporary thing, and since you're not going to have it forever, it's important to work it while you can and live out the natural born queen inside of you to the fullest! So that once you are gone, you will leave behind a warm glow.

Take your place in the sun, because the war has been won. We are free to be whatever and whoever we want to be. And I love it.

Chapter 18

The Pinball Wizard

When I first found out about doing a duet with Elton John I was in a hotel in Los Angeles, and after putting the phone down I screamed nonstop. I ran around my hotel room for about five minutes screaming. When I'd composed myself, I picked up the phone again. When I was told that Giorgio Moroder would be producing, I went through the whole process all over again—dropping the phone and screaming some more. A duet with Elton John and Giorgio producing! These were two icons, two legends whose careers I knew inside and out—and I was gonna get to work with them both. I was the luckiest drag queen alive.

But the question was, what song should we do? Some

months earlier I had been bashing around the idea of doing a cover version of a song for the *Supermodel* LP, perhaps even doing a duet. "Don't You Want Me?," originally by the Human League was one suggestion, and "Don't Go Breaking My Heart" was another. In the end, I did neither, opting for "Everybody Dance" by Chic instead. But when the question came up about what song we were going to do, the answer was obvious.

Me and Elton.

Elton was an absolute doll, and so was Giorgio. We recorded in Atlanta, so I felt at home. It didn't take long to record the vocals. While Elton and I hung out and gossiped, Giorgio ran off a rough mix of the track. That night Elton invited me to his boyfriend's for a family picnic, where he presented me with a portrait of me he had bought at an art gallery in Atlanta, and we talked for hours. Being with him was so easy, I felt I had made a new friend.

Elton was really happy with the track, and he decided that it would be his next single. He also decided that there should be a video for this. I was disappointed when he said that he wanted the same people who had made all the other

RuPaul videos to make this video, because that was my management team. Now as much as I love those videos, I wanted my managers looking after me instead of being busy directing a video. I had also hoped for something much bigger: more time, more costumes, more money.

But since they wanted it done quick and cheap, we came up with the idea of having me and Elton re-create some famous couples in history: Sonny and Cher, Antony and Cleopatra, and the pair from the famous *American Gothic* painting. Adam and Eve, Ike and Tina Turner, Tarzan and Jane, Superman and Lois Lane were other ideas that did not, alas, make it past the storyboard stage. The beauty of this concept was that the whole thing could be shot in the six hours Elton was going to make himself available to us in a studio with a blue screen. It was also a neat, simple device to showcase the fun chemistry between me and Elton, without a lot of time-consuming business and sets getting in the way and cluttering things up. Believe it or not, it all went very smoothly.

I think this will always be one of my favorite videos because of the final scene. I am completely obsessed by the movie *Grease*. It has the fun and lightness of the fifties, but a knowingness of what happened after that in the sixties and seventies. Sandy is so innocent at first and starts out with the purity of the fifties. But then she leaves all that behind and becomes a hot-rod chick in the end. It's filled with all these sexual innuendos; I know what *you* want to do. And the music is fierce! Altogether it's total camp, a fantasy of everyone coming together free, wild, and uninhibited, and all thanks to the music.

Anyway, I've always wanted to re-create that moment at the end of the movie when Olivia and John Travolta wave goodbye. I've watched this movie about a hundred times, and each time I always wave back at the television set at the end. I've also always wanted to play Olivia Newton John. I know her every line, every move, and every nuance in that movie like the back of my hand. So I was really excited about re-creating that waving scene.

Don't Go Breaking My Heart:
the video.

There was just one hitch, Elton agreed to do all the famous couples. Except *Grease*. We went ahead and got the costumes anyway in the hope that once we were over in London I could persuade him. And I did.

Mind you, in terms of coups it really is a toss-up between getting Elton to do John Travolta or Marie Antoinette. When I first met with him in Atlanta, he proud-

ly showed me his latest photos as Sharon—his drag persona. He was in a hotel in Hawaii looking devastating in an enormous hat with a bold floral pattern. I got the impression that he was very keen to do drag in the video, but that his management people were less keen. So we were never quite sure until the last moment if Marie Antoinette would ever appear on the set. When he finally did, he was so bound and tied—those *Dangerous Liaisons* costumes are very constricting—that he could hardly move, poor thing. Once he ditched the Little Bo Peep stuffed lamb and staff, he made a fantastic Marie Antoinette. And it was a thrill for me, too, because I got to do male drag for a change, as the Sun King Louis XIV.

Elton was a total pro. In between takes we entertained ourselves by playing Spotlight. This is a game where you make your opponent an object. Then they get to ask you questions to try and figure out what you've made them. At the beginning of the day we started out with normal, inno- cent objects—I made him a Rolls-Royce, and he made me a bird fountain. By the end of the shoot, we were turning one another into colostomy bags and boogers. It was the fastest video I've ever done. He was a joy.

The single was scheduled for release on Valentine's Day, which also coincided with the Brits, England's equiv- alent of the Grammys. Elton was asked to present this prestigious awards show—which was carried live on nationwide television—but on condition that I was his co-presenter.

Naturally, I was thrilled but anxious; I only had one nerve left—and it was sciatic. Sciatica is an extremely unpleasant and painful back condition where sharp pains shoot down the backs of your legs, even if you are just sitting still. It had been bothering me for some time but suddenly became chronic. At night I would just lie in bed crying with pain. I really missed my mother then, because I would have liked to just call her up and say, "Mom, it hurts so bad." And I knew what she would say, too, "Ru baby, run a hot bath and put some Epsom salts in it and soak in that." I could hear her voice playing in my head, and that was comforting. Still, there was no way I was going to do the Brits. In the end I relented. I didn't want to let Elton down—he had been so good to me.

When I arrived I spent a couple of evenings with Elton—one at his house in Windsor, which is like an old museum. Even Elton doesn't know how many rooms it has. As he took me on a tour of the house, we stumbled across a room that housed what was left of the famous Elton John eyewear collection,

on display in glass cases. I had never seen so many eyeglasses in all my life. He explained that these were the ones that had too much sentimental value for him to part with. The house contained everything you could imagine: an indoor pool, a fitness center, and millions of dollars' worth of art and antiques. The tour ended on a balcony that was a stone's throw away from Windsor Castle. Elton's other house in London is more contempo-

rary. It is smaller, although it too has its own fitness center, pool, and every imaginable luxury as well. Both homes are gorgeous, and every room is filled with fresh flowers.

Elton was always very sweet and solicitous. One time at his house in Windsor, he asked me where my boyfriend was. I explained that he wasn't with me this time because he doesn't like appearing as "the boyfriend." He listened and he said "You know, I've had that problem my whole life with relationships because of who I am, and people feeling that they don't have an identity when they're with me." I told him that I've had a problem with men my whole life starting with my father. We talked about this, and I felt we really connected, he also having come from a broken home.

On the day of the Brits my sciatica was throbbing, so the chauffeured Daimler assigned to me had to take me first to an osteopath named Dr. Bender. I was in so much pain I could barely stand up. After the doctor did his thing, it was off to Alexandra Palace, where the Brit Awards were to be held. Once we got there they brought in a masseur who laid me out on the floor of my trailer. The show was to open with Elton and me singing "Don't Go Breaking My Heart." Just as I was about to make my grand entrance,

1. Cloris Leachman: Check her out in *Young Frankenstein,*
High Anxiety, and *The Last Picture Show*
2. Joan Collins: A real movie star. One of my favorite comeback stories.
3. Faye Dunaway: She rules in *Network* and *Chinatown,* not to
mention *Mommy D.*
4. Susan Sarandon: From *The Rocky Horror Picture Show* to
The Client . . . brilliant.
5. Geraldine Page: In *Sweet Bird of Youth* and *Summer and
Smoke,* she is truly transcendent. A great American actress.
6. Cicely Tyson: Go head on, Miss Jane Pittman!
7. Agnes Morehead: A fabulous film history before
"Bewitched."
8. Beah Richards: Everybody's favorite aunt. She plays
Diana's in *Mahogany.*
9. Thelma Ritter: Pops up in every film made in the fifties.
10. Diana Ross: Nominated for an Oscar for her acting debut,
Lady Sings the Blues. The Boss can act.
11. Marilyn Monroe: Underrated as an actress. Check out *The
Misfits.*
12. Mildred Dunnock: Fierce on stage and screen.
13. Joan Crawford: What can I say, the woman's acting style is
pure Kabuki theater.
14. Cathrine O'Hara: I wish I could see more of her.
15. Joan Cusack: She rules in *Working Girl.*
16. Bette Davis: Need I say more?
17. Jan Hooks: Funny, funny, funny . . .
18. Lizbeth Scott: Greatest speaking voice on film.
19. Eve Arden: Give me *Mildred Pierce* any day.
20. Gena Rowlands: You must see *Another Woman, Gloria,*
and *Woman under the Influence.*
21. Carol Burnett: When I was at Bob Mackie's studio, I tried
on a fat suit she wore in a skit. What an honor.
22. Edie McClurg: Give this genius her own television show . . .
please.
23. Elizabeth Taylor: I could watch *Who's Afraid of Virginia
Woolf* every day for a year.
24. Whoopie Goldberg: The most unlikely movie star. A true
inspiration for all.
25. Alfre Woodard: She's up there with the greats.
26. Grace Zambrinsky: Weird and wonderful.
27. Diane Ladd: Truly a trip in *Wild at Heart.* Must see *Alice
Doesn't Live Here Anymore* and *Ramblin' Rose.*
28. Rosalind Russell: A delight in everything she did.
29. Anna Magnani: She makes you feel her every emotion.
Rent *The Rose Tattoo* and *Bellissima.*
30. Jennifer Jason Leigh: In *Single White Female* she used the
perfect murder weapon—a stiletto heel.
31. Madeline Kahn: I lose myself laughing at *Blazing Saddles,*
but she's phenomenal in everything she does.
32. Carroll Baker: I live for her in *Baby Doll.*
33. Vivien Leigh: Drop dead gorgeous. See *The Roman Spring
of Mrs. Stone.*
34. Grayson Hall: *Night of the Iguana*—what a nut!
35. Ginger Rogers: A legendary dancer, but an unrecognized—
and excellent—actress.
36. Audrey Hepburn: Pure joy.

waves of sharp pain shot through my body. I thought I was going to pass out, fall down the stairs, and arrive on stage a bag of bones in a beautiful mess. But I didn't, and the song went off just fine.

In between awards I would hobble off, pray for the pain to go away, and get into another costume. Changing costumes was about the only thing I had to do other than read all the double entendres that had been scripted on the TelePrompTer. I am convinced that there is one script-writer from hell who writes all award shows all over the world. For example, only a few months earlier I had been on the *Billboard Music Awards* telecast presenting an award with Queen Latifah. "Ru, congratulations on win-ning the best maxi single sales award of 1993," she said, to which I was to reply, reading from the TelePrompTer, "Baby, it was the best *twelve-inch* maxi single sales award." Then she had the punch line, "Honey, I'm not going to *touch* that one." Ho! Ho! Ho! I may be a drag queen, but why does that mean all I am interested in is stupid dick jokes? It was no different with the Brits. The Pet Shop Boys opened the show by laying on this spectacle of 200 Welsh miners wearing mining lamps and singing the vocals to "Go West" by the Village People. Genius. After the number, as the miners went offstage, the line on my TelePrompTer was, "I haven't seen so many helmets in my whole life," making a joke on helmets, which in England—only in England—means the same thing as "head," as in "tip of penis." Talk about lame. A critic wrote that I did not understand the humor—too right!

In the end, it was all worth it. The single went to num-ber 7 in the British charts and did some action in Europe too, which necessitated flying off—by private jet—to Italy and Germany to do some gigs. I loved doing the San Remo festival in Italy. We had a police escort to and from the air-port, with sirens blaring as we raced up one-way streets the wrong way and drove on the pavement just to get to the sta-dium on time.

Chapter 19

Public Domain

A part of my fame has nothing to do with me. I came along at just the right time. After Reagan, the pendulum had swung so far over to the right that my arrival signaled that it was crashing all the way back to the other side. People were curious, opening up, and no longer wanted to be held hostage by their prejudices and assumptions. Spring was in the air!

Because I am not the sole and exclusive author of this process, I have been able to watch it one step removed. That's why I often think of myself in the third person, not because I think I am royal—although I am a queen—but because I see RuPaul as a product. The RuPaul experience is rather like a ride in a theme park: You put a quarter in the slot and off I go.

At every step of the way during this fantastic voyage, I have been like a kid in a candy store. My progress as a star has been a series of milestones, and as each one has gone by I've said to myself, now I've *really* made it. And then the next one comes along. On one level there are the obvious ones that are indicators of reaching a certain saturation—performing on Pleasure Island at Disney World in Orlando (I have always thought of Mickey and me as soulmates), or doing MTV's Spring Break at Daytona (they ran and ran that thing).

On another level it has been the things that seem the most trivial that have meant the most to me. Like having my own Winnebago for the *Supermodel* shoot. Of course after San Remo, I am satisfied with nothing less than presidential-style motorcades with police escorts. Then there was the time I first saw a RuPaul poster up on the street, a poster that I had not put up there myself. That was so overwhelming for me, I had to run inside, grab my video camera, and tape it. As I was doing this a friend came by and asked me what I was doing. When I told him, I think he thought I had lost my mind. After that you can imagine my reaction when I saw my very own billboard on Sunset Boulevard in Los Angeles. I stood across the street and looked at it for about half an hour—people thought I was crazy then too, because no one hangs out on the streets in L.A. I think I actually cried with happiness. Another one of those sweet moments was when I went to Bloomingdale's to do something or other, and there was a mannequin of me in the window. Then there was the time my UK record label put up huge life-size posters of me in bus shelters. They were always very generous and spent a fortune on promotion. But they really outdid themselves when they released "House of Love" as a single. For the cover they did a Warhol-like portrait of me à la Jackie O. and Marilyn Monroe. At last, I had my own Warhol!

Generally, this whole process of turning into a pop icon has been a lot of fun. I've been used as a punch line for jokes on TV shows like *Martin, Fresh Prince, In Living Color,* and *Saturday Night Live.* Then there are the less welcome bits, like becoming part and parcel of Howard Stern's routine. One week he thought I was a hot mama, then the next week he'd poke fun at me because I wouldn't go on his show. (What self-respecting person in their right mind would?)

Somewhere along the line, though, the stakes got a lit-

In my trailer on the set of Crooklyn. *I played the bodega woman. Spike Lee was warm and generous, contrary to how he was portrayed in the press.*

tle higher, and I realized that I was losing control of the whole process. The press started making up stories—complete fabrications. Beyond a certain point they have to, because after the first story—"She's a He!" (which was in fact the page-three headline in the *National Enquirer*)—what are you going to say? One of my favorites is in the *Weekly World News* with the headline "Disco Diva RuPaul tells 400 fans to get lost." According to the paper, RuPaul showed up out of drag at a video rehearsal and demanded that 400 faithful fans be taken out of the theater because he didn't want them to see him like that. Well, obviously, with what we know about RuPaul, RuPaul would never do that.

Another favorite was the reported fight between me and Boy George, in a nightclub, where he was supposed to have actually ripped my wig off! That was in the British press, where they care even less about facts than in America. On the eve of the Brits, the *Sunday Mirror* printed a piece about my supposed sleazy past as a star of porno films. They ignored the fact that my films like *Voyeur* and *American Porn Star* were avant-garde comedies and treated them as if they were the real thing.

It can be scary. Sometimes I feel like I've sold my soul. But most of the time, I just laugh it off and resign myself to the fact that it is all part of the deal of becoming public domain.

And that's why I feel I have never changed. I've al-

Off duty supermodels: me and Linda Evangelista.

The making of A Shade Shadey *video.*

ways conducted myself as a star. Always. When I was down, I was simply, from my point of view, a superstar in exile. When the rest of the world didn't know I was a star, I conducted myself as one, believing that sooner or later the rest of the world would catch up with me. That was why it was funny for me to see people treating me as less than a superstar, because they didn't know any better. But then when superstardom really did come knocking on my door, nothing really changed except other people's behavior toward me. People who wouldn't give me the time of day were all googly eyed over me. I know what it's like to be down and I know what it's like to be up, and I know that there's no real difference between the two. The only thing that changes is your point of view, and that you can always change. It's a question of mind over matter.

The truth is that success is something between you and your own butthole. Only you know how far you've come. Only you know how far you want to go. Only you know what lesson there is to be learned. This journey is my journey, the highs and the lows, the successes and the disappointments. So whatever it may mean to other people, it means the world to me, because it's mine, and no one can ever take that away from me.

Chapter 20

A Goddess Struggling to Be Born

Everything I know today, and the most important lessons I've learned, were all learned the hard way—through life's painful experiences. The rest I got from television. For example, when I was twenty-eight and living in L.A., I had been in showbiz for seven years and had nothing to show for it. I had no money, couldn't get a job. I couldn't even get arrested. I spent the holidays holed up at my mother's house watching television. And as fate would have it, PBS was running the Bill Moyers series *The Power of Myth* by Joseph Campbell. At the end of the six-hour series I knew it was kismet that I was there in the place of my birth to watch it.

One episode in particular struck a chord with me. It

was all about the goddess, and how, because we live in a masculine culture, her energy hasn't been evident for about

Me at my family reunion. With my family's blessing, I knew I could conquer the world.

two thousand years. It helped me realize that with the harmonic convergence, the Wall coming down in Germany, the end of the greed decade, and people recognizing their spirituality, that the goddess energy was making her comeback now.

Watching that program also made me realize that I should not despair, because I was a part of that energy, and that there was a place for me in her revival. It helped me see the woods as a whole, so I was no longer lost among all the trees.

My energy is goddess energy because of my ability to open myself up to people. That's my feminine side. I'm nurturing to people. I am approachable. I don't bite, and so it's easy for them to approach me: "Come to me, my hands are open, I will not hurt you, you are welcome here." That's my forte.

In today's masculine culture, hiding our emotions and our feelings is seen as a sign of strength and power, whereas being loving and giving is seen as a sign of weakness. In the presence of the goddess the opposite is true. Strength is being loving and giving. Feminine energy has very little to do with being effeminate. It is not soft and frilly.

Which is more important, the bee or the flower? On the one hand, there's the bee, busy and buzzing away with typical male aggressiveness. On the other hand, there's the flower, lying back and letting the bee come to it to get the pollen. The flower opens up to let this happen. In our society we think that the bee is more power-ful and important. But the bee's work can't be done with-out the nurturing flower opening up and saying, "Come to me." There's tremendous power in that surrender, in being the nurturing one.

The eighties was trouser-wearing, ball-breaking, go-getting at whatever cost and at whoever's expense. But this is the nineties. We've had enough of the masculine. It's abrasive to us now, and we don't like it anymore. We are welcoming back femininity, goddess power, and we want that—we're thirsty for the nurturing.

I believe it's the only way we can save this world and our planet—by letting the goddess blossom inside each one of us. To do that we have to unlearn the lessons that a love-less world has taught us.

My mom said you can't trust men and you can't trust people in general. She taught me how to be fearful of them. She said, "People take kindess for weakness, Ru." And so, as a defense mechanism, we learn how to regulate our love. We learn not to open up, and not to show our true selves because people will use that against us. This is how we deal with being in a loveless culture. We put on armor to pro-tect us from people who will take advantage of us.

When we see children and animals we say, "Come on, come here, I love you." We love them so much because we recognize the part of ourselves that's been supressed, and we never really lose that part of us, it's always there. Or if someone falls, our natural instinct is to rush over and help them without a second thought. It's our natural essence to love and perpetuate life. But along the way we learn these loveless behavior patterns—that's the way of the world as we know it today.

But starting today, that must change. It's all about coming full circle. That's what being reborn is. You're born into this world full of love and wonder. Then you learn the ways of an unloving world. The next step is to be reborn into what you were initially, which is loving and full of wonder. This process is no different from the evolution of Christ, Buddha, and Krishna. And this is the process that every living thing must experience.

That's why we need teachers. I'm just getting my education right now, but the education I got in school—what was that? That was *not* how I got my education. School should teach you about the existence of your soul, how to feed and nurture it. It should teach you the importance of gazing out of the window, how to channel that energy and where to go when you do. But, instead, school is like prison, and all it really does is suppress the imagination and kill off your curiosity.

I wish they taught this lesson to children at the beginning of school, but from a very early age we are taught that we are not really clean unless we are Zestfully clean. All we learn in school are the ways of the material world, basing self-worth on what we can acquire. Instead of learning about love, all we learn about in school is about shopping, about going to the mall. We learn about how to enslave the soul and how to enslave our brothers, by buying and selling things, buying and selling each other. But we can only go to the moon so many times, we can only do so much and buy so much. My sisters would tell me when I was growing up that in the future everybody in our society was going to have eight pairs of shoes. The idea was that The People In Charge are going to make it better for the other people, and I said, "Yes! hallelujah! Eight pairs of shoes!" As I got older and discarded my Mary Tyler Moore-isms I realized that it wasn't going to happen. The Fat Controllers are only making it better for themselves. If they have their way they will have eight million pairs of shoes, and everyone else will have to go without.

The reason *The Wizard of Oz* had such a profound effect on me was that Dorothy has to go all the way to the end of the yellow brick road to realize that she already had what she had been searching for inside of her. So, as I got older, I began to realize that the final frontier was not outer space, it was inner space.

I see this time as a time of transition, a sort of interim stage. I call it the Age of Oprah. The Age of Oprah is about everyone finding that part of themselves that's special. An initial part of that process is to go through a cleansing. One way of doing this is going on television and talking about all your stuff, and as a country we seem ready to talk and spill the beans. Recently on *Ricki Lake* they had people coming on and revealing major secrets on the air. This pregnant girl came on and said to her husband, "Honey, I got something to tell you . . . Darling, the baby I'm carrying—it's not yours." Why would someone do that on national television? I'll tell you why—they're cleansing the parts that Zest or any other deodorant soap cannot reach. The Mayans used to sacrifice one another in front of the gods, the Polynesians used to throw themselves into the mouths of volcanoes, and we, to cleanse ourselves, go on daytime talk shows and confess. It's all part of America's craze for twelve-step programs. This trend is really quite recent. When I was a kid there were all these things I wanted to talk about with people, but no one was 'fessing up. I said to myself, "Why aren't people talking about these things?" Well now they are—and with a vengeance!

I have to say that when I became an adult and got out into the world, I thought I was such a damn freak. But now, having watched a zillion episodes of *Oprah,* and having

heard what other people's lives are like, I feel quite ordinary. But taking my cue from Oprah, my goal is to open up more, and show more of myself—show my depth. I don't want to be an imitation of Oprah, but in the way that Oprah is herself—undiluted, unadulterated—that is what I want to work on.

And I think doing that is going to take one more chapter, at least.

Cover shoot for Paper *magazine.*

Chapter 21

Big Daddy

Being a man attracted to other men has never been a problem for me. It's just the way I am.

When I was eight I had an abdominal hernia operation. I remember being in the hospital, getting in the wheelchair, and going to the bathroom. In the bed next to me there was this guy who was eighteen or so. He had a broken leg, and it was up in traction. As I passed by I looked over, and he had nothing on underneath his robe. Obviously, it wasn't the first time I had seen a man's penis, but the emotional jolt took me by surprise. My heart was racing. Up until this point everyone else had told me I was a sissy, now I was making the connections for myself.

About a year later, I had a similar eye-popping experience with an older boy. Bernie, a neighbor, must have been about sixteen when he took it upon himself to be my big brother. Like me, he had older sisters, and wanted to make sure that I had a male influence. For about three years he would take me places on his motorcycle, like down to Tijuana looking for whores. But I wasn't interested in them, I was interested in him. One day I saw him getting out of the shower, naked, and I thought to myself, "Wow!" My mouth just dropped open because he was so beautiful. He still is. Gorgeous.

But in spite of these experiences, I was still quite naive. One time when we were stoned and talking about sex, my best friend Albert said, "I'm really horny right now," and before I could say Jack-in-the-box, he whipped it out to prove it. He had a massive hard-on, and I couldn't believe how big it was. I think he wanted me to do something about it, but all I could say was, "That's not your dick! That can't be real!"

When I was older I started going to the gay center, where I made friends with a counselor named Raymond. We would meet once a week, twice a week, whenever we could get together, and talk about gayness. One day he said, "Would you like to kiss me?" That was the first time I ever really kissed a man, and he was a good kisser. I felt my knees buckle. I left the planet. He was thirty-six, and knew I was a virgin, so he said if you want to have sex, you've got to wait until you're eighteen. The next two months, until my eighteenth birthday, crawled by. The day after I went to his house. It was my first time.

Soon afterward he left town. Left to my own devices, I started going to the local gay club. I was a little nervous at first, because I had never really done that before, but I soon became a staple on the scene because the music was so good: "Relight My Fire" by Dan Hartman, "Dance Disco Heat" by Sylvester, "Heaven Must Have Sent You" by Bonnie Pointer.

Then I met this boy in Balboa Park, the local cruising ground. He was a sailor named Johnny from Pine Bluff, Arkansas—an all-American boy. He was twenty-one and

had brown, brown skin, and sandy hair. He was really cute.
I would go pick him up at the navy base and we went out
for about a month, having sex in the back of my mom's car.
But then he broke up with me because he was religious,
and having sex with another man did not work for him.

It was never an issue with my folks that I was gay—it
was just assumed. It was common knowledge. I was
always flamboyant. So to say, "Hey, I'm gay" to my mother would have been like, er, duh! My mother used to make
fun of me and say, "You're a punk, you're a sissy," but it
was never like, "When are you going to get a girlfriend?"
It wasn't until years later, after a devastating relationship,
that I started thinking about how I dealt with men. My
mother would always say, "You can't trust men," and that
was something all us sisters learned from her. Whenever it
came to boyfriends, it was always, "Oh, men! Oh my God,
no!" So one day I called her up and we had a real good
heart-to-heart all about it.

My father did talk to me about being gay one time.
My sister Renae warned me that this was going to happen
because someone told him they had seen me in Balboa
Park. Sure enough, my daddy called and said, "Ru, I need
to talk to you." So we went into the park and he said,
"Ru—this lifestyle—you'll be very lonely." I cut to the
chase and said, "This is not something I've chosen, this is
something that I have always been." And that was that.

But it wasn't. Because what I didn't tell him was that
I thought, "How dare you come into my life now and tell
me about being lonely, when you left me alone all those
years ago?" You see, I don't remember very much about
him being around, or being there for us as a father.

He always used to say, "Remember your family. You
need to know who your cousins are, Ru, so that if you need
them they'll be there for you." Meanwhile, when I needed
him, he wasn't there. He said that he loved me, but he wasn't
there for me when I needed him. So he sent me a message
that love is painful and that you can't trust people who say
they love you.

When he lived with us he was very strict with us. He

would put pork rind cracklins in the cornbread and make us eat them. I hated that. But when he moved out of the house, he was always very sweet. He loved to laugh, had a great sense of humor, and loved to tell jokes.

After my parents divorced, my father moved to Los Angeles to live with his girlfriend Betty and went to work for the people who make Skippy

My father served in the Korean War. I look more like him than anyone else.

peanut butter. He had visitation rights and would spend weekends with us, which consisted of him taking us down to Tijuana to get my haircut for fifty cents. Then he would take us to the Agua Caliente, the horse races. Mexico wasn't very far away from where we lived, and on a clear day you could see Mexico from the front door of my house. We were always coming back across the border with cheap liquor under the trunk. He would say, "Okay you kids, when Border Patrol ask you your nationality, you say 'USA.'" After they had looked in the trunk or whatever, they would point at each of us and we would say, in turn, "USA," "USA," "USA." They never caught us because they weren't bothered about a few bottles of booze—they were looking for drugs and illegal aliens.

Dad was a big gambler, and he was also very unreliable. He was always late. He would say, "I'm going to pick you kids up at eleven." Twelve o'clock would pass, one, two—no Daddy. We'd sit on the porch waiting and playing games betting that the next car that went past would be Daddy's. We'd count cars coming by, but it would never be him. Sometimes he would show up later that night and be drunk. Other times he'd never show up at all. That was my father's modus operandi, and it's taken me a long time to deal with it.

My mother would say, "He ain't no damn good." I really did not want to believe that, but after years of her reiterating it, and after years of him never being able to keep his word, I simply couldn't help believing it.

So throughout my life I've always had a problem with men, because I never trusted them. The child inside of me is still there, and is still holding on to my experience of my father's shortcomings as Truths. But the past is the past, and I don't want to project it on the future. So it's simply a matter of telling the child, "That's not how it is. That may have been him, but that's not everybody."

So, I grew up believing that everything that was male was rotten to the core, even my own maleness. I felt my father had betrayed me, and my reaction was to shun my maleness because I thought that was him, and part of his legacy. I didn't want anything to do with it. I denied my manhood and thought that it was a bad thing.

Now that's over with. I've since forgiven my father and that has enabled me to move on. I've become my own father, not my father who is my real father, Irving Charles, but my own father in terms of for myself and being the man in my life that I never had. I feel comfortable with my masculinity really for the first time.

A psychic helped show me the way. She told me that my father and I had shared past lives together. This is how she explained it: When I appeared in this life, my reaction to him was, "Hey, buddy, how are you doing? Don't you remember, it's me?" But his reaction to me was, "I cannot see you because I cannot see myself, and I cannot love you, because I cannot love myself." My response to that was, "Let me help you, let me remind you who you are. You want sorrow? Here's some of mine. You want love? Here, I have plenty. I can make you laugh, I can sing for you. Whatever you want my spirit will merge with yours, and you can be how we used to be." But he could not see that. So, in essence, I spent a lifetime trying to get his attention, trying to get him to acknowledge me, and never receiving the acknowledgment I wanted so badly.

This scenario with my father continued when I

started to get into relationships with other men. Men just like my father. Very beautiful and charismatic, but unable to give me the love and approval I ached for.

At school, when I was eleven, I had this friend named Danny, and that was the first time I fell in love with someone. Although he wasn't gay or anything, I think he liked me a lot, but he wasn't in love with me. One day he came to pick me up for school and my mother answered the door and cussed him out, as usual, and she said, "Get your fucking ass away from here, what are you doing?" Later that day at school he was devastated. So from then on I went to visit him up in his neighborhood, which was across the freeway. After a glorious year with him in seventh grade, he decided to go to another school. I *had* to be with him, so I followed him out to Lewis Junior High. It didn't work out for me. He was into a whole other world, and had a girlfriend and everything. So I went back to my old school with a broken heart. But I still carried a torch for Danny for years afterward, even later when he was dating my sister Rozy.

Looking back, this marks the first of many relationships I had with men who didn't love me the way I loved them. Throughout my school years I fell in love with other

Rozy's wedding. My whole family together at last—except for me. From left to right: Renae, Daddy, Rozy, Mama, and Renetta.

straight boys, and it seemed like the same hopeless scenario as with Danny. It took me years to realize that I was just repeating this scenario again and again and again. I kept on falling in love with men who were unavailable to me for reasons I could only trace to my father. In my subconscious mind, if a man was distant but kind to me, I couldn't help falling in love with them, because I knew they couldn't love me back, and Danny was the first in a long line of men who fit this description.

For example, the second time I took a hit of acid I was in Atlanta. I did it by myself and went for a walk that led me directly to the park where the water was. That's where my voice was telling me to go. It led me directly to a group of young kids, one of whom, Christopher, would become my first real boyfriend. The moment I saw them, I started doing my California thing: "Hey, guys, how you doing?" and they were like, "What's this?" They were all about two or three years younger than me, but when I saw Christopher, it was love at first sight. I had never felt this way before. I sat down on the swing next to him and our knees met. I could feel the vibrations coming from him, and he (as he later told me) could feel the vibrations from me. He was about six foot three, very skinny with fair skin and dishwater blond hair, crooked teeth, and a huge nose. Very redneck-looking. Even to this day I think he's gorgeous.

That summer was the summer of love for me because we fell in love in a big way. We were inseparable, and eventually moved in together. Christopher and I lived together for six months off and on. We had fights galore and broke up and got back together. Then broke up again, and then got back together again. He was very distant and emotionally remote. I on the other hand was the complete opposite. I liked to talk things through, and get things out in the open.

Rather than face the music, Christopher would run off to Athens, Georgia, to be with friends. We'd make up and he'd come back home. This happened so many times, it was embarrassing. But, eventually, we faced the fact that our summer of love had become a winter of discontent, and we finally split up at Christmastime. I was devastated. I couldn't stop thinking about him. I was obsessed with him, and, just as with Danny, it took years for my obsession to fade.

There were other relationships in between, but nothing so profound. I didn't make sense of the deep, deep pain until years later when I fell in love with someone born on the exact same day and the exact same year as Christopher. His name was Jack. I fell in love with him at first sight also, and this was the summer of '89. By now I was beginning to decipher the pattern, and this relationship unfolded almost exactly like the others. He pursued me and we had a wonderful summer together, and as I returned his affection, he began to back off. All that year we went through the wringer together. We were friends for three months, and then not speaking for three months. Ultimately, and bitterly, our relationship ended. If I had been devastated in the past, this time I felt annihilated.

With no other choice, I was determined to break the chain. I was determined not to live in limited love. I was determined to figure this problem out. I could not understand how I felt such deep feelings for someone I had known for only a few short months until I retraced my steps back to the wounds of a seven-year-old left unattended. I learned that the feelings I had were not necessarily for Christopher or Jack, but the deep pain I felt for my father, feelings that I had transferred from my father on to them. As a child I had pushed those feelings deep down inside because I was simply unable to deal with or even understand them. In this way I just deferred them. Finally, I got to dig them up, and instead of just feeling the scale of the pain as I had in all my relationships to this point, I got to understand the nature of the pain.

The pattern was that I went after men who fit the emotional scenario set up years before by my father. Like well-cast actors, they were perfect candidates to fill the void left by him. The role called for fear of intimacy and emotional distance, and that explained why I was never interested in the men who made themselves available to me. Once Jack turned cold, I was hooked. It felt like home, it must be love. Wrong.

I have always gone after people who are aloof and distant. The more I go for them, the more they back off, as if to say, "No, I can't have love, 'cause I don't love myself."

My mother's funeral. From left to right: Rozy, Daddy, me, my niece Morgan, Renae, and Renetta.

And then I perpetuate the lovelessness, because when someone does that to me—comes on strong—I react in the same way by stepping back and going, "Wait a minute! No! I would not want to be in a club that would have me as a member." It's a vicious circle I had to escape from. A person can love you, but they can only love you as much as you allow yourself to be loved.

It was not until I forgave my father by resigning myself to the fact that he was incapable of giving me the love that I always wanted from him that I was able to move on and accept love from men who were willing to give love to me. As I look back, there were always men who were interested in me—but I wasn't interested in them. Because if I let them love me they would threaten my deep conviction that I could not be loved. I would be busted!

Now that I have forgiven my father, I can see that for all that my mother said about him, he was not the loser she portrayed him as. Today he lives in his hometown of Mansfield, Lousiana, where he runs a beauty supply house, of all things. In spite of that, we don't have much in common. We don't have the kind of communication where we sit down man-to-man or even human-to-human and really talk about things.

I talked to him recently, and he told me about how a whole vanload of kids pulled up outside his house because there was a rumor that I was going to be there for Thanksgiving. And they were saying, "You RuPaul's daddy? You RuPaul's daddy?" He said he was, but they weren't having it. "You ain't RuPaul's daddy. How he so tall?" He said something about my mother and my grand-mother being tall, so then they said, "Well, if you is RuPaul's daddy, dance for us." He said he could not dance, and they said, "How you can be RuPaul's daddy if you can't dance?" So, you see, he's very charming and usually controls the conversation by laughing, telling jokes, and trying to keep it light. And when you try and steer the conversation in another direction or get serious, he gets very evasive.

He likes to keep things on the surface, and I'm fine with that now. Everyone has their own agenda to work out, in their own time, and if he knew of a better way to deal with his emotions he would do it. I can really forgive him, understanding that he did the best he could with what he knew. If he could have done it better, he would have. As we all would.

As the years have passed, both Christopher and Jack have come to me independently and sincerely apologized for not being emotionally available. They realize that it's an ongoing problem in their relationships as well, so they are growing too. And I got to apologize to them too, because I wasn't perfect then, and I'm still not. None of us are. That's why we're here. We're here to learn and to grow.

The way for me to grow is by listening to my gut. Any question you may have you can answer by listening to your gut. That's where your knowledge is. In your gut. That's the part of you that's real. That's you.

For my part, I still haven't totally broken through, and I have a lot to learn. But I feel that I'm beginning to understand my own power and I'm ready to reclaim the love that I have put on the back burner.

I used to base so much of my life on what other people thought of me. I have a sense of myself and a security in knowing that I am my greatest asset.

Whatever happens, I'm going to be fine. I have no fear. So I can actually go on and live my life and be myself; be the man that I am, be the woman that I am, the everything that I am.

Afterword

I was cruising at 33,000 feet, and wondering if I could get any higher than this.

I have been a world traveler for eighteen years. I've been on every kind of transportation: planes, trains, automobiles, tractors, cars with flat tires, bicycles with one wheel. You name it, I've ridden it. But there I was returning from a whirlwind tour of Europe—Frankfurt, Paris, Rome—about to make a connection to catch the Concorde.

Unless you're taking the space shuttle, it don't get no classier than that.

Looking out of the window, I saw the Matterhorn below—a rock of ages fierce in its mantle of snow. And I thought, "I am that mountain. I am the Matterhorn." All right, I admit it, I was on monkey time. In fact, it was worse than monkey time, I was on gorilla time. First stop Germany was where I turned out the Wiener schnitzel yet again, the next stop was Paris, where I performed at Club Queen; and then, with hardly any sleep, it was on to Italy for another gig. By the time I made it to the airport lounge you had to scrape me off the floor to get me on the plane.

Me and choreographer Kenny Ortega on the set of To Wong Foo, Thanks for Everything . . . With Love, Julie Newmar.

It was all such a mad rush because I had to get back to the States to shoot my role as Miss Rachel Tensions in the Spielberg drag flick, *To Wong Foo, Thanks for Everything . . . With Love, Julie Newmar.* The script called for me to be lowered on a swing onto a runway in a New York nightclub to crown one of many hopeful drag queens as the new Queen of New York. The three drag queens vying for the crown were to be played by big Hollywood stars. This movie had been the talk of the biz for some time, because agents were worried about their superstar clients letting their hair down as drag queens. After much toing and froing, it was decided that Wesley Snipes, Patrick Swayze, and John Leguizamo would play the three leads.

I was looking forward to meeting this famous trio—especially on equal ground in wigs and heels. Beneath all the gloss, glamour, and stardom, I am just a regular Joe who is a major fan of almost every star in the galaxy. That's one of the best things about being just slightly famous—it's like having an all-access backstage pass. I can get to meet all the people I have been fans of all these years. And although I've met many of them—from Mariah

Carey to Barbara DeAngelis, from Janet Jackson to Latoya Jackson—in the firmament of stars, there is really only one person I have always been dying to meet.

When I entered the Concorde lounge, I idly wondered to myself what star I was going to meet that day: Would it be Linda, Naomi, Christy?

Then all of a sudden I heard a voice so dear to me and so familiar, that on hearing it my hands started shaking and my eyes welled up with tears.

No! It's not! It can't be!

I was frozen to the spot, unable to turn round. I could neither bear the disappointment if it wasn't who I thought it was, or face her if it was. I simply was not ready to meet—the ultimate star!

"I would like to be in the front row," said the voice.

That voice! It had to be! It couldn't be!

"Can you make my seat number 1A, please?"

It was! It was! I knew it was her.

Finally I could trust myself to look up without fainting away. She was sitting directly across from me, by herself, wearing a brown pant suit, hair down, no makeup, and sunglasses. She was reading *Marie Claire*.

It was all I could do to stop myself from screaming out loud.

After about ten minutes I felt strong enough to walk, so I got up and went to the bathroom, where I prepared myself to take the plunge.

Poolside at the Chateau Marmont in Hollywood.

On the way back to my seat, I stopped to say hello.

"Hi Diana, I'm RuPaul. How are you doing?"

"Oh my God! I thought you looked familiar."

"I would have come over earlier, but I didn't want to bother you."

"Oh, don't be so silly, sit down, sit down."

Immediately, we started chatting like girlfriends. I told her about the film.

"If it's Steven, you know it's going to be good."

I told her about how I had met her daughter Tracee on an audition for a Keenan Ivory Wayans movie, and she told me that she was working for *Mirabella:* "I wish they would be doctors and lawyers, but there they are, in the business."

"I tried to catch Rhonda at Tatou, but I missed her," I said. Her daughter had a singing engagement at the famed Manhattan nightspot.

"That's right—she's not playing there anymore."

Then we talked about her other daughter, Chudney, who is at Georgetown and into rowing.

We chatted away, but I could tell that she wanted to ask me something. When she did, it was about my wigs and how I got them to look so realistic. I told her that I shave my head and have a collection of lace-front wigs.

"Oh, of course!"

We both laughed and then talked about her music and recording, and I asked her why she wasn't doing a whole album with Luther Vandross.

"Oh, I want to, but it hasn't worked out due to scheduling."

Supermodel summit.

After about ten minutes of this a little girl walked up and asked her for an autograph. I could not resist.

"While you're at it, can I have one too?"

"Of course you can. But what shall I sign it on?"

I tore a page out of my Filofax. I also had my Polaroid with me and suggested we take a picture together.

"Oh, but I look awful."

Lies! She looked great!

"Write your address down for me and I'll send you one."

I dug into my Filofax and found a Polaroid of me, scribbled down my address, and handed it over.

"Wow!" she said, "You look beautiful—your teeth are gorgeous."

At that point, Vernon Jordan of the NAACP walked by, and they started talking.

Diana introduced me and he said, "I'd never have recognized you." At that point I decided to excuse myself—*Style with Elsa Klensch* was on CNN.

"It's okay, you don't have to leave," she said with a smile. I was on Cloud Nine.

And then Robert De Niro walked over.

Diana began to introduce me, but he said, "I know Ru, we met at a Luther Vandross concert"—as we did.

He was on his way back from vacation in Bali. We chatted about film, and I asked him how you ever forget about the camera with it right there in your face. He said it was the director's job to make you forget about the camera and your job to keep your focus. Here I was getting acting tips from Robert De Niro. He asked me if I was into doing anything out of drag, and I explained that I fully intended to work the man and the woman in me. He got a kick out of that.

Then it was time to board. The plane itself is quite ordinary—small and narrow, and the food no better than regular first class. But the glamour is wall to wall, and everyone was dripping with diamonds, making it the twenty-first-century version of the *Orient Express*. As De Niro walked past me—he was in the seat behind me—he patted me on the the shoulder, and the person sitting next to me said, "Gee! you must be famous."

Taking off on the Concorde is very much like any other plane, except that when you hit cruising altitude, the sky outside is deep, deep blue. Looking out of the window, you can see the curvature of the earth, and so, although you can't feel that you are going faster, you get this interplanetary rush, the feeling that you are traveling to outer space.

After a while, I had to use the ladies' room, which was just forward of the front row. It was in use so I had to stand outside for a min-

The costumes that Bob Mackie made
for my first stint in Vegas.
Cher and Tina, eat your hearts out.

ute—right by Diana. She was looking in her bag to see if she had any Alka-Seltzer for a passenger who was feeling air sick, but she couldn't find any. As I walked by she said, "Uh-uh, I'm next!"

We chatted for a minute, talked about her latest projects, and I suggested that she should do an updated version of *Auntie Mame* with all new songs.

"Not only are you gorgeous but you are very talented too," she sparkled.

I was already God knows how many feet off the ground, but this just sent me into orbit. As she said this she whipped out the Polaroid I had given her and showed it to the passenger sitting next to her. He whistled quietly and said, "You are so beautiful!"

"Honey," I said, "you ain't seen nothing yet—just wait until you see my legs."

In the end, she let me go first because she said I was so tall. It was just as well since the person who had been in there before me had made kind of a mess. I wiped down the seat and basin for her. Honey, I would have scrubbed that place spotless so she did not think that *I* had made that mess.

In no time at all we were in New York. Diana went to change currency and walked into baggage claim all by her-self, with just a skycap in tow. All the while I was watch-ing and thinking how organized and how self-sufficient she seemed.

And then it was time for our farewells.

"Bye," I said.

"Bye, honey."

Walking on air, I headed straight to the set.

Finally, my dreams had been eclipsed by my reality.

RuPaul's U.S. Discography

RuPaul: "Sex Freak"—Vinyl/LP—Funtone, 1985—(Freak 23)

RuPaul: "Starrbooty—Motion Picture Soundtrack"—Vinyl/CD—
Funtone 1986 (Every 23)

RuPaul: "Ping Ting Ting"—Vinyl 12" single—Funtone 1987 (DV 23)

RuPaul: "Starrbooty's Revenge"—CD/Casette—5 Years of Funtone
Compilation 1990 (Fun23)

RuPaul: "I've Got That Feeling"—Vinyl 12" single—Cardiac 1991 (3-
4011-0-DJ)

RuPaul: "Supermodel/House of Love"—Vinyl/CD/Cassette and 12"
maxi-single—Tommy Boy 1992 (TB 542)

RuPaul: "Back to My Roots/Strudel Model"—Vinyl/CD/Cassette and
12" single—Tommy Boy 1993 (TB 565)

RuPaul: "Supermodel of the World"—Vinyl/CD/Cassette LP—Tommy
Boy 1993 (TB 1058)

RuPaul: "A Shade Shadey (Now Prance)"—Vinyl/CD/Cassette 12" sin
gle—Tommy Boy 1993 (TB 578)

RuPaul: "Little Drummer Boy"—Vinyl/CD/Cassette 7" single—Tommy
Boy 1993 (TB 7593)

RuPaul/Elton John: "Don't Go Breakin' My Heart," Duets—
Vinyl/CD/Cassette LP maxi-single—MCA 1994
(MCAD/MCAM 54796)

RuPaul: "What You See Is What You Get," Addams Family Values
Soundtrack—CD/Cassette—Atlas 1994 (295920025-
2cd/295920025-4cassette)

RuPaul Music Videography and Videos That Feature RuPaul

Love Shack: B-52's

Some Robert Palmer video—can't remember the name

Good Stuff: B-52's

Supermodel (You Better Work): RuPaul

Back to My Roots: RuPaul

A Shade Shadey (Now Prance): RuPaul

Little Drummer Boy: RuPaul

Don't Go Breakin' My Heart: Elton John and RuPaul

RuPaul Filmography

Starrbooty: Jon Witherspoon

Starrbooty II: Jon Witherspoon

Starrbooty III: Jon Witherspoon

Trilogy of Terror: Jon Witherspoon

Terror 3D: Jon Witherspoon

Wild Thing: Tom Zarilli

Connie Francis Story: Wayne Hollowell

Mahogany II: Wayne Hollowell

American Porn Star: Wayne Hollowell

Psycho Bitch: Wayne Hollowell

Voyeur: Wayne Hollowell

Police Lady: Wayne Hollowell

Police Lady II: Wayne Hollowell

In Ferno: Ellen Von Untwerth

Just Between Girlfriends: Jon Witherspoon

Crooklyn: Spike Lee

To Wong Foo . . . : Beeban Kidron

Brady Bunch: Betty Thomas

Shantay: Randy Barbato and Fenton Bailey